Why RACISM Still EXISTS
In America with Asian Americans

Dr. Herbert K. Naito

Copyright © 2024 Dr. Herbert K. Naito

ISBN (Paperback):   979-8-89381-087-5
ISBN (eBook):   979-8-89381-086-8

All rights reserved. No part of this book may be reproduced
or transmitted in any form or by any means, electronic or mechanical, including photocopying,
recording, or by any information storage and retrieval system, without permission
in writing from the copyright owner.

The views expressed in this work are solely those of the
author and do not necessarily reflect the views of the publisher, and the
publisher hereby disclaims any responsibility for them.

508 West 26th Street KEARNEY, NE 68848
402-819-3224
info@medialiteraryexcellence.com

Table of Contents

Something About the Author 1

Chapter 1 Introduction.. 2

Chapter 2 Demographics of Hawaii 4

Chapter 3 Arrival of the Chinese Immigrants 8

Chapter 4 Arrival of the Japanese Immigrants... 23

Chapter 5 Arrival of The Korean Immigrants.. 43

Chapter 6 ASIAN-AMERICAN CASE STUDIES 57

Chapter 7 Multi-factorial Causes of Asian Racism 77

Chapter 8 Possible Solutions to Asian Hate Crimes.................................. 81

Chapter 9 Summary 132

Notes 148

The US Review of Books.. 150

Something About the Author

He is a graduate of the University of Northern Colorado with a BA and MA degrees in biological sciences and with a certified teaching certificate in secondary education in Colorado. He also has a PhD degree in physiology from Iowa State University and a Master's degree in business administration from Lake Erie College. He was a Clinical Professor of Clinical Chemistry at Cleveland State University Graduate School of Chemistry (And board certified) and Clinical Associate Professor at the Ohio State University School of Medicine.

He served on the medical staff at The Cleveland Clinic Foundation as a Senior Scientist and published over 150 peer-reviewed scientific papers in medicine. He was also on the medical staff at the Department of Veteran's Affairs in Cleveland, Ohio as Head of Clinical Chemistry and Point-of-Care testing. He is current on the Board of Directors at the Mercy Health Foundation in Youngstown, Ohio.

He was invited to Who's Who in the Midwest, Who's Who in America, Who's Who in Frontiers of Science and Technology, Who's Who in Society, Who Among Asian Americans, Who's Who in Science, Who's Who in Science and Engineering, and Who's Who of the year. He is also listed in American Men and Women of the year, American Biographical Institute (ABI) Most Admired Men and Women of the Year, ABI Most Admired Man of the Decade, International Biographical Center (IBC) International Man of the Year, IBC international Man of the Year, IBC International Who's Who of Intellectuals, ABI Five-Hundred Leaders of Influence, National Association of Distinguished Professionals, and Covington Who's Who Top Executive of the Year.

He is a third-generation Japanese American that was born and raised in Hawaii-an international-multicultural community. He gave lectures in every corner of the world on heart disease, which gave him the opportunity to observe and study how people of different skin colors get along with one another.

This book was supported by a generous grant from the Dr. and Mrs. Herbert K. Naito Charitable Foundation.

Chapter 1
Introduction

The Merriam-Webster's Dictionar^{36} defines *RACISM* as "a belief that some races are by nature superior to others; also, ***discrimination and prejudice*** are based on such belief and others."

Worldwide, racism still exists today. In America, hate crimes still exists among many cultures today. In fact, there is an increase in discrimination today, and perhaps into the future. Throughout American history, White Americans have generally enjoyed legally or socially sanctioned privileges and rights which have been denied to members of other various ethnic or minority groups at various times. European Americans, particular affluent White Anglo-Saxon Protestants, are said to have enjoyed advantages in matters of immigration, voting rights, citizenship, land acquisition, criminal justice proceedings, and education privileges. Racism against various ethnic or minority groups has existed in the United States since the colonial era. Native Americans have suffered genocide, forced removals and massacres. African Americans were enslaved during early American history and continued into modern times with severe restrictions on their social, political, and economic freedoms. Latin Americans, Hispanics, Middle Eastern, Pacific Islanders, Asian Americans have also been victims of discriminations, prejudices, racism and hate crimes— even today. These hate crimes prevailed with non-Protestant immigrants from Europe—especially the Jews, Italian Americans, Irish Americans, Polish Americans, and many other nationalities of color.

Racism in America has manifested itself in a variety of ways— including discriminatory practices, genocide, immoral-socially unethical judicial laws, and slavery with segregation laws, isolation of races into Native American reservations, internment camps, physical beatings, hangings, and the like.

According to the *United Nations* and *Human-Rights Network*, discrimination and racism extend to all walks of life—especially to people of color.

Why?

Is it because they look different?

Is it because they have different cultural customs?

Is it because they belong to a certain social-economic level?

Is it because they have a certain educational level?

Is it because they belong to a certain religion?

Is it because they live in a certain housing development? Is it because they belong to a certain political party?

Is it because they speak a different language?

Is it because they eat unusual foods (i.e., Organ meats like tongue, tripe, chitlins, fish eyeballs, and chicken feet)? Or is it because of their skin color?

Skin color is only a one millimeter deep—once removed, you have the same muscles, bones, and blood vessels. The only difference is how you think, your attitudes, your beliefs, your needs, your goals, your aspirations. Thus, every person is unique and deserves respect for their individuality.

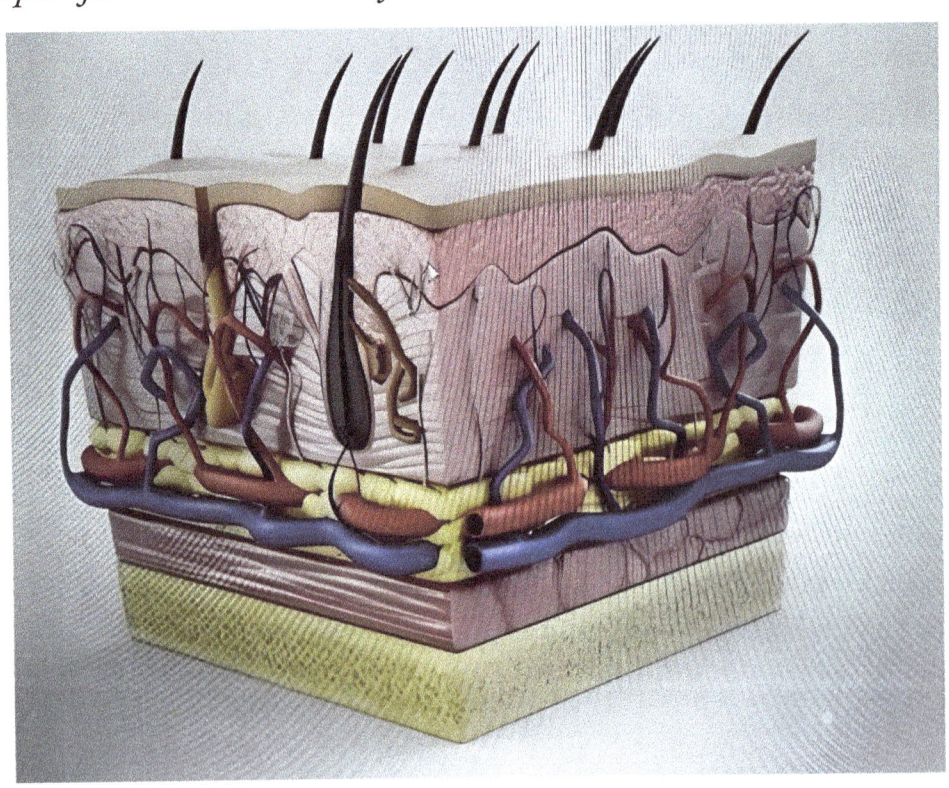

Photo 1. Anatomy of the human skin. Why do people make a big deal of skin color? It is only 1 millimeter deep (the thickness of tissue paper).

Chapter 2
Demographics of Hawaii

A. What does Hawaii—The International Melting-Pot of America has to offer?

If you want to experience less racism, move to Hawaii according to Moises Velasquez-Manof[1] Race might be perceived differently in Hawaii compared to the mainland United States. The University of Hawaii (Manoa Campus) has an ongoing study on how kids view kids of other races (Intergroup Social Perception Lab Studies). Given the critical role that psychological essentialism is theorized to play in the development of stereotyping and prejudice, scientists have increasingly examined the extent to which and when children essentialize different social categories. They reviewed and integrated the types of contextual and cultural variations that have emerged in essentialism depending on experimental tasks, participated in social group membership.

Caucasians comprise the largest racial/ethnic group in Hawaii (40%), followed by the Filipino (25%), Japanese (20%), and Chinese (10%), others (5%)[2] This makes Hawaii the most multicultural state in the Nation. Nearly 25% of all residents identify with more than one race as compared to Alaska (7%) with the next most the Asian subgroup, Japanese students comprise 9%, Chinese students account for 3%, and Korean students are only 1% of the student population. When combined, African Americans (3%), Native Americans/Alaskan Natives (0.6%), and Hispanic students (4%) comprise less than 8% of all Department of Education (DOE).

Americans/Alaskan Natives make up the majority of the different races. Nearly 27% of the student attending Hawaii Public School are Native Hawaiians, 22% are Filipinos, and 16% are Caucasian students.

Among one of the fastest growing sub-populations in Hawaii's public schools is Micronesians (4%), who came from the U.S. Pacific Islands.

The racial and ethnic diversity of students at the University of Hawaii differs from the racial and ethnic diversity of students in the DOE. The Caucasian-, Chinese-, and Japanese-American college students represent the majority. It becomes more pronounced at graduation with Causations (31.7%), Japanese-

Americans (10%), Chinese-Americans (8.0%), followed by Filipino-Americans (4.2%) and Korean-Americans (3.0%). These statistics do not represent the thousands of students from Hawaii to attended colleges and universities on the U.S. mainland and in other countries. African- Americans have the lowest four-year graduation rates of all students. I mention these statistics because education may be key to preventing racism. The next topic in Section B: is on how research can prevent to this unwanted behavior.

Photo 2. The inhabitants of Hawaii. The majority are mixed of culture (Called hapa in Hawaiian).

B. **How can the University of Hawaii—The College of Inter-racial Studies teach other colleges and universities throughout America about racism?**

The ongoing studies at the University of Hawaii—*The Intergroup Social Perception Lab Studies on Hawaii's children* will be a key data base to help formulate methods to reduce racism. This information will be critical for government to formulate anti-racism plans and laws for the future. The data should be shared with other colleges and universities that are gathering similar data to formulate a white paper so debates can occur with other experts to resolve this issue.

Photo 3. The University of Hawaii—Manoa campus. East-West campus on International Studies.

C. Set Up an Internationally Renowned Commission on Racism Led by the University of Hawaii and Supported by Other Universities with Similar Goals.

The data from other institutions of higher learning should be harvested to form a White Paper on Identifying the causes of racism and discrimination and provide possible solutions on resolving the hate crimes worldwide and in America.

Once this platform is established, the commission can be formulated to conduct symposia to hear the voice of the public and political leaders with power to introduce new anti-color laws and eliminate archaic laws that hinder the progress of racism and discrimination.

This is only the BEGINNING! It may take several generations of mankind to observe significant of this movement.

Figure 1. Emblem of the State of Hawaii; motto: "The Life of the Land is Perpetuated in Righteousness."

Chapter 3
Arrival of the Chinese Immigrants

To seek a better economic life the Chinese Immigrants started to migrate to Latin America—Cuba, British West Indies, British Guiana, Trinidad, Jamaica, Mexico, Brazil between 1838-1917 as plantation workers (419 Chinese men), 140,000 Chinese men went to Cuba, 90,000 more went to Peru to enter the hard, bitter labor force. Chinese women and their wives were left home back in China. By today's definition the Chinese-men laborers were treated like slaves. They were then called "Coolies" or indentured laborers by Caucasian- wealthy men living in Hawaii, bound under contract.[2, 14, 37] The Chinese began to arrive in America beginning 1820s. They came by the thousands to join the hard labor force, which was defined as *slave labor,* back in those days.

On the other hand, migration of Chinese men to Cuba and Peru was part of an unregulated multinational business involving the transport of both indentured (a written certificate) or non-indentured workers while African slavery was still in effect in these two countries. Many of the laborers were recruited through kidnapping, coercion, and deception. This led to high mortality rates because of the high disease rates due to the lack of caring of their health—a criminal injustice. Beginning in the nineteenth century the Chinese immigrant laborers migrated to America when they heard of "The Gold Rush." They were required by law to fill an affidavit with the U.S. Federal Bureau of Investigation stating that they intend to travel back to China and return to the United States—required only by the Chinese Immigrant culture! Beginning in 1882, the United States passed a series of Chinese Exclusion Laws that barred Chinese laborers from entering the Country and allowed only certain "exempt" classes of merchants, students, teachers, diplomats, and travelers to enter or reenter America.[1] After protest from the Chinese American Community, the Chinese-American citizens were allowed to apply for admission or readmission. However, all Chinese living in the United States were under strict surveillance. They were required to fill out a number of government forms, subject themselves to interrogations and investigations, and provide affidavits from two White witnesses who vouched for the Chinese Immigrants and their status each time the left or reentered the Country.[1, 3, 39] The unfairness can be found with Chinese immigrants living in this Country for over 20 years and still had to apply for the government application to leave and renter America. While the 1898 U.S. Supreme Court challenge affirmed the constitutional status of birthright citizenship for all persons born in the United States (regardless of race), Chinese Immigrants had to carry a *"Certificate of Identity"* at all times. Many found that their Chinese citizenship status offered little protection from discrimination of race. Discrimination was keenly felt among the 2nd generation Chinese Americans who grew up by adapting to the American ways, found little protection from being able to live like an American. In 1913 and 1923, politicians introduced bills in Congress designed to disfranchise citizens of Chinese ancestry. The *Immigration Act of 1924*, explicitly excluded "aliens ineligible to establish citizenship (a reference to all Asians) and the *1922 Cable Act* revoked the citizenship of women who married "aliens ineligible for citizenship." The victims of this discriminatory law were Asian American women who married Asian male immigrants. Once a woman lost her citizenship, her rights to own property, vote, and travel freely were revoked.[1,3,39]

Photo 4. A Chinese immigrant woman dressed in a traditional dress.

Furthermore, on February 28, 1892, Senator John Miller of California introduced a bill, *The Chinese Exclusion Act*, to the U.S. Congress to exclude Chinese-Immigrant laborers from this Country because Chinese Immigrants came from a "degraded and inferior race." Other Senators jumped in to compare the Chinese to "rats, beasts, and swine.[1, 3, 39]"

During the late nineteenth and early twentieth centuries, many Chinese Immigrants came as laborers, known as *"Gam Saan Hack"* or Gold Mountain men.³ Their wives were forbidding from traveling abroad; they were expected to take care of their husbands' parents and perform filial duties of their absent husbands. The U.S. immigration laws presented some of the most formidable barriers to female Chinese immigration. The 1875 Act barred Asian women suspected of prostitution as well as Asian laborers transported to the United States as contract laborers.

Eligible women of age and wives of husbands living in America illegally entered the United States to join their husbands.³, ³⁹ Many White American citizens took the opportunity to capture these illegal immigrants and made them sign a contract for *human trafficking*. In the San Francisco area, an illegal Chinese woman went for a high price ($400) to a slave dealer, which was equivalent to purchasing a car back in the 1930s! A small number of Chinese prostitutes became concubines or mistresses to wealthy Chinese men. Some Chinese prostitutes escaped from their contracts. Some were able to turn to Christian missionary work, like the Presbyterian Mission Home, which claimed to have rescued 1,500 women.*1, 39*

By the 1850, there was a small community of Chinese immigrants who worked as street peddlers, cigar makers, laundrymen, cooks, laborers in the agricultural fields, restaurant owners, Chinese grocery store operators, and as other merchants.

While most of the Chinese immigrants married their own kind, there were a minority who married other races and cultures, i.e., Irish Americans and Europeans. ***The Expatriation Act of 1907*** decreed that any American women who married a foreign citizen would lose their citizenship. This law removed the intermarriages between Asians and Americans.³

The anti-Chinese sentiment grew more violent as time went on; beginning in the 1850s – 19ᵗʰ century, Chinese were systematically harassed, rounded up, murdered, driven out of cities. A massacre of Chinese took place at Rock Springs, Wyoming during September 1885. On October 24, 1871, seventeen Chinese were lynched in Los Angeles when a policeman was shot by a Chinese suspect. A mob of 500 went on an attack and dragged Chinese out of their homes while others hastily built gallows downtown Los Angeles to hang the victims—which would become the largest-mass lynching in U.S. history.³, ³⁹ Over 300 Chinese Immigrants in Eureka, California were arrested after a city councilman was accidentally killed in a crossfire between two Chinese gang rivals. On September 2, 1885, 28 Chinese Immigrant men were killed and another 15 were wounded in Rock Springs, Wyoming; hundreds of others were driven out into the desert.*1, 3, 39*

By the end of the 19th century, Chinese Immigration was a central issue in Hawaii because of the many diseases that they carried. The transplanted missionaries from the U.S. mainland were an especially dominant force in shaping public opinion about Chinese Immigration in Hawaii. However, during the 1870s and 1880s Canada and America to prevent the Chinese Immigrants from entering.*3, 39*

The Chinese-Immigrant labors for the transcontinental railroads numbered in the thousands—all under *slave labor* conditions. Many died in the bitter, wintery weather—right in their footsteps to be later picked up to send their bones back to China. Many Chinese Immigrants refused to work under those inhumane conditions. They were paid half the amount of the White laborers. They eventually went on strike. They were whipped and beaten. Many did not survive the harsh weather conditions, bitter cold, lack of nourishment and food. Be mindful that the Chinese understood what hard labor was all about in China and knew how to survive the hard labor when they emigrated to United States. Hard labor was in their life's blood. In addition, many Chinese immigrants were good businessman.

Photo 5. For the Chinese culture, the Chinatown (San Francisco, Ney York, Chicago) is their safe heaven; everything is located there, including their friends and family—which is why it is their social hub.

Photo 6. Chinese immigrant Transcontinental Railroad men workers who were treated unkindly and horribly because of their skin color and customs.

What about the Asian children? They did NOT want to see all the mistreatment and horror that they observed.[6] They are hurt and sad; they wanted you to see beyond the differences. Color creates differences, which should be beautiful. More is written about these special group of people in Chapter 9.

Why is there so much hatred?

Why is there so much jealousy when they worked so hard at such low wages?

Photo 7. Chinese immigrants working long hours in the onion fields in California; often called slave labor.

A. The Family Unit:

In an ideal Chinese home, three generations (Grandparents, parents, and children) of the same family live under one roof. The head of the household was the grandfather or eldest male. The Chinese family unit is based on[3]:

Photo 8. Chinese family eating traditional food with chopsticks.

- *Patrilineal*—the term means that descent was calculated through men. A person was descended both parents, but one inherited one's family membership father. The Chinese people were extreme in that a woman was explicitly removed from the family of her birth and affiliated to her husband's family. Reverence was paid to ancestors. For a male, this referred ancestors and their wives. For a female it referred to her male ancestors and their wives.

- *Patriachal*—means that the family was hierarchically organized with the prime institutionalized authority being vested in the senior-most male. He was considered to be responsible for the orderly management of the family unit. No two family members were equal in authority. So, a family was run by a man. Decisions were made by one male and not collectively by husband, wives or children like many other societies.

- *Prescriptively Virilocal*—means that there was a strong belief that the newly married couple should live with the groom's family.

- *Kinship Group*—means that the members of the family were related genealogically either by having common ancestors or by being married. A family is not a household, but rather included tenants, servants, apprentices, priests, adopted individuals, and others in the building.
- *Sharing a common household budget*—is strictly an economic way of sharing the family budget that crossed several house-hold. This is certainly unique to the Chinese culture.
- *Inheritance*—Since the family unit of ownership (Even down to the level of sharing toothbrushes), there was nothing that quite corresponded to inheritance. The many U.S. laws that guaranteed Chinese women inheritance was strongly resisted by the Chinese men.

The strong institutionalization of the family Chinese unit would seem to have made it more important and central in that society than in most societies[3].

Photo 9. Chinese immigrants at Angle Island working at slave labor wages.

B. The Chinese Immigrant Culture:

The saying, "family is Life," is certainly is true with the Chinese culture. In fact, it is very, very important to the point that their value system is influence by Confucian religion. Today, some Chinese Immigrants and Chinese Americans still believe that love is shown through the provision of money to one's family members. Less focus is being put on personal bonding as parents work harder and harder to earn more money for their family members.

The Chinese culture is unlike the Japanese or American cultures, whereby they were fostered by other cultures. It grew gradually out of its own independent development. It has distinctive charectristics.[3]:

- Chinese culture has its own features and its unique systems like its writing system, legal system--which are radically different from those of other cultures. The Chinese, Indian, and Western cultures are generally acknowledged to be the world's three great distinct cultural systems because each has its own structure.
- While ancient cultures were counterparts to Chinese culture, such as Egyptian, Babylonian, Indian, and Greek cultures either disappeared or were transformed or lost their national independence, only Chinese culture still survives today, having ensured its status as an independent nation has remained interrupted.
- It can be observed from China's past history that from the very beginning Chinese culture has possessed the greatest capacity to assimilate with other cultures and absorb their advanced elements without being subject to any transformation itself.
- China has been able to integrate its neighboring countries and other ethnic groups into the huge nation it is now. It can be said that Chinese culture not only exceeds all other cultures in longevity but also goes beyond them in space. That is to say, the huge unified society which has grown out of Chinese culture boasts a huge percentage of the worlds' population.
- In its enduring life span, the Chinese culture witnessed a lack of change or progress, especially in recent centuries. This seems to show that Chinese culture boasts a huge percentage of the world's population.

- The impact of Chinese culture upon its surrounding areas is both great and far-reaching. Its sphere of influence has reached worldwide.

C. Role of Confucianism Religion:

Photo 10. The Confucius religion deeply affected the Chinese culture and way of life.

Confucianism is a system of philosophical and ethical teachings founded by Meng Ke, who lived from 372 to 289 BC3. Included in his teachings are: are the love for humanity, ancestor worship, reverence for parents, and harmony in thought and conduct. There are four main principles:

1. Respect for Autonomy
2. Beneficence
3. Non-maleficence
4. Justice

Like Japan and Korea, Confucianism had a major impact on the Chinese culture, which existed for over 2500 years. Confucianism strongly emphasizes:3

- Ren—is the central ethical principle, and is equivalent to the concepts of mercy, love, and humanity.
- Social order—there are five cardinal relations (Called *Wu lun*):
    a. *Sovereign-subject*: The family is the center and comes before the individual.
    b. *Father-son:* The father is the undisputed head of the family; what he says becomes family law. With regard to filial piety (Xiao), sons, especially the oldest son, have specific obligations toward the family and are expected to respect and care for parents.
    c. *Elder-younger brother:* The older brother's responsibility is to help and guide the younger brother.
    d. *Husband-wife:* The husband is the head of the household and is responsible for fending for the wife.
    e. *Friend-friend:* The proper way or *Li*, includes a set of rules for interaction with others and the role system. Control of emotions, restraints, obedience to authority, conforming and "saving face" are highly valued and important in Chinese society.
- Fulfillment of responsibilities—Confucianism was the affirmation of accepted values in primary social institutions and basic human relationships. All human relationships involved a set of defined roles and mutual obligations.

Role of Education:

Photo 11. Chinese education was stressed a little less early than the Japanese or Korean cultures.

A well-educated workforce is instrumental to technological and scientific discovery, which can propel states to the apex of the increasingly innovation-based global economy.

The most notable Chinese government policy is the *1986 Law on Nine-Year Compulsory Education*, called for achievement of the two basics' universal enrollment among school-aged children (6-15 years) and full literacy among those under the age of 20 year.[3, 31, 39] Despite this effort, education in China remains uneven. Students born in Beijing or into affluent families generally had greater access to higher-quality education as compared to lower-income families. Initially Chinese focused primarily on hand labor technology, unlike the Japanese or Korean cultures—99% and 97.9% literacy rate, respectively.

High levels of literacy serve as the foundation for improved access to information and directly enhance an individual's ability to contribute to society. As of 2011, China had all but eliminated illiteracy among the young and middle-age citizens! Latest statistics indicate that a city like Beijing has a 98.52% literacy rate during 2014 as compared to students from the rural areas.[3]

Most of the Chinese Immigrants that went to the U.S. for work were from the rural areas of China with a lower literacy rate. By 2003, Whites had the highest literacy rate, followed by Asians/Pacific Islanders. The Blacks and Hispanics followed. The brutal murder of Vincent Chin by two unemployed Detroit autoworkers galvanized the Chinese-American community. The tragedy solidified the movement devote their lives to political activism. Many Chinese Americans learned from painful experiences that American education (Even public education) was not a right for their children, but a privilege that had to be fought for. In 1859, San Francisco school board making no secret of their contempt for the Chinese (Referring to them even as "baboons" and "monkeys"), shut down a public school for Chinese children, even their parents were required to pay school taxes along with other residents of the city.[3] Under public pressure, authorities reopened the Chinese school, but passed state laws in the 1860 to segregate Asian, American Indians, and Blacks from the White public school system. For 14 years (1871-1885), Chinese children were the only racial group to be denied a state-funded education. The Chinese community made desperate appeals to the school board to admit their children into the public schools, but these were repeatedly ignored. Finally, the Chinese Americans turned the course in 1884; Joseph Tape, an interpreter for the Chinese consulate, and his wife, Mary, a photographer and artist sued the San Francisco Board of Education when their daughter, Mamie Tape, was denied admission to a public White primary school.[3] Today, Asian-Americans attend prestigious Ivey-League schools, private colleges and universities because of their parental strict upbringing— making their children extremely fierce and competitive in high school, especially in math and in computers. About 60% of the students that attend top universities are Asians. The Asian students are statistically overrepresented in the best American universities. That happens because they tend to be, on the average, more intelligent than Americans of other races.

The Effects of War:

Even as they struggled to find work, Chinese laborers in the U.S were fighting for their lives on two fronts: (1) due to discrimination and (2) due to fighting in the Civil War and World War II.

Although the *1862 Act of Congress* promised U.S. citizenship to any honorably discharged foreign veteran, Chinese Americans were denied that right because an earlier law allowed the naturalization of Whites only. There were many Chinese who served in the Civil War and in the regular U.S. Army after the war for a decade or two, but were still denied U.S. citizenship. Many Chinese men came through the *Pacific Slave Trade*, adoption by Americans, independent immigration, or influenced by missionaries.[3]

In 1882m Congress passed the Chinese Exclusion Act, which until 1943, made it technically illegal for Chinese living in America to become citizens of the United States of America[3].

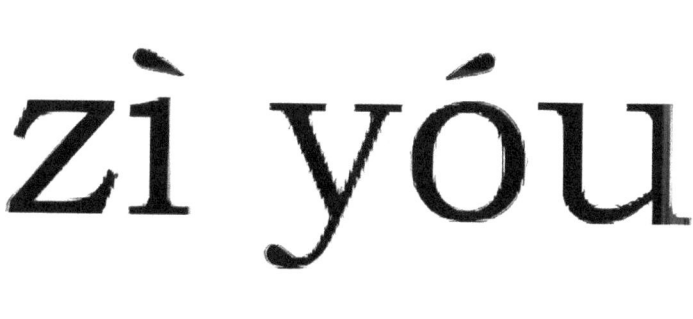

Figure 2. Chinese word that translates to Freedom.[5]

Chapter 4
Arrival of the Japanese Immigrants

Photo 12. Japan had a Civil War in Japan from 1868 to 1869, often called the "War of the Year of the Yang Earth Dragon" or the Japanese revolution. There were three warlords during that time, but it was Lord Tokugawa who unified Japan for over 200 years.

Japanese immigrants, or issei (1st generation in America), were the second largest group of Asian immigrants to come to America. Between 1885 and 1924, about 400,000 Japanese migrated to the United States to seek work and the fortunes[7]. They were mostly young, male *dekasegi* (Temporary traveler) who actually remained in America and did not return to their homeland as originally planned. They settled down and called for their families to join them to build strong ethnic communities in Hawaii and states along the Westcoast.[7, 28]

During the early 16th century, small numbers of Japanese began immigrating to other countries, such as Portugal and Brazil to farm. The Japanese government during 1639, implemented a policy of isolation to protect Japan from European colonialization spreading throughout Asia.[7] It did allow trading with China and the Netherlands; however, it banned Japanese from migrating further until 1858.

Labor recruiters and traders quickly established themselves in Japan to send workers to Hawaii's sugar plantations. This emigration of young Japanese men was sent to Australia, Fiji, Philippines, Mexico, Peru, Canada and USA for hard labor. Due to the high taxes that the Japanese farmers were enforced to pay, over 300,000 were forced to sell their farms.

Photo 13. A young Japanese girl with a traditional Kimono on.

On January 20, 1885, the first group of Japanese immigrants boarded the *City of Tokyo* cruise ship bound for Honolulu.[7] They included 666 men, 158 women, 69 boys, and 48 girls.[7] Between 1885 and 1924, over 200,000 Japanese went to Hawaii and 180,000 went to the continental U.S. Even though it was expensive to travel to a Hawaiian plantation ($100), the laborers could earn four to six times more—establishing economic security for the future in the United States.

Future immigration of Japanese laborers was prohibited by the *1908 Gentlemen's Agreement* between Japan and America. However, from 1891 to 1900, 27,440 Japanese male laborers, were admitted into the United States. Over the next seven years; 52, 457 more Japanese laborers (Mostly young males) were allowed into America. Another 38,000 came from Hawaii until President Theodore Roosevelt signed an Executive Order in 1907 banning aliens from entering the continental United States via its territories like the Pacific Islands. The Japanese immigrants filled jobs that the Chinese immigrants once had (Mines, lumber mills, railroad construction, fish canneries, sugar cane fields, pineapple fields, and domestic servants.[7] The 1909 census showed 40,000 Japanese immigrants worked in agriculture, 10,000 on the railroads, and 4,000 in fish and pineapple canneries[7].

The Japanese immigrants did not remain laborers forever; many turned to agriculture (Vegetables, fruits, and nuts) as they decided to reside in America. They purchased small plots of farm land or leased fertile land. One-Japanese farmer arrived in the San Joaquin Valley during 1887 and grew potatoes and after several years saved enough money to leased a small plot of land (To harvest potatoes) that soon expanded to a large operation near Stockton, California. By 1926, his estate was worth 15 million dollars[7]. Thousands of other Japanese Americans followed in his footsteps by working hard, using good business ethics and management to gain the trust of Americans by excelling in customer satisfaction.

As they began to establish themselves economically, Japanese Americans also formed tight-knit communities in the USA. They formed economic associations to pool their resources through a rotating credit system and farming cooperatives to buy supplies and market crops. From the 6th to the 8th centuries, Chinese cultural and political influences entered Japan via Korea and profoundly influenced Buddhism, the Chinese script, and Chinese methods of government.[24] The most famous administrator of this period was Prince Shotoku (573-620 CE) who introduced his *Seventeen Articles of Constitution*, based on the Chinese system of government, and with it a concept of the state; Buddhism was also established as the national religion. In the 300-year period between the mid-1500s and mid-1800s there were two turning points in Japan's history.[24] The first arrived in the form of Christianity, brought by the Spanish Jesuit ministry, St. Francis Xavier, during a two-year period during 1549 and 1551. The second turning point was essentially a response to Japan's total withdrawal into total isolation following expulsion of the Christians. The Shinto religion took over during 16381868. Essentially there is no ethical content to Shinto religion, although there is an emphasis on ritual purity that might reflect the Japanese love of bathing and high regard for personal hygiene. Washing of one's hands and mouth in necessary before entering a Shinto shrine. The Shinto priest often with the support of shrine maidens (Or *miko*) usually had four aspects of worship: purification, offering and worship, supplication and prayer, and preparing the participants to communicate with the *kami*--for placing requests and wishes.

There were growing background noise of racial discrimination among the Japanese Americans during the 1900s. Japanese Americans efforts to be fully accepted as Americans were largely unsuccessful. The Japanese became targets of discriminatory laws at the local, state and federal level to prohibit Japanese from becoming naturalized citizens. For instance, Japanese were denied membership into mainstream labor unions. Worse yet, the treatment they received were less than dignified because of their looks and skin color. After the war, the physical, mental and verbal abuse were horrific, demeaning, undignified, and cruel.

When Japan attacked Pearl Harbor on December 7, 1941 at 7:59 AM, all Hell broke loose. Japanese Americans were gathered and thrown into internment camps that were built in:

Photo 14. Japanese attack bombers bombed Pearl Harbor on December 7, 1941.

Photo 15. Japanese attack bombers bombed Schofield Army Barracks and air fields (Located in the middle of the island).

Pinedale, California

Pomona, California

Central Utah

Colorado River, Arizona

Heart Mountain, Wyoming

Granada, Colorado

Jerome, Arkansas

Minidoka, Idaho

Rohwer, Arkansas

Tule, California

These concentration camps were built to house Japanese immigrants and Japanese Americans in barbed-wired fenced barricades, many with machine-gun towers to prevent the prisoners from escaping.

Photo 16. The Japanese-American citizens were thrown into internment camps (A kind word for prison camps).

The food provided to the Japanese - American Prisoners were unfitting to eat. The cold winters were unbearable because of the lack of blankets for warmth in uninsulated huts. There were no heaters installed in the barracks. Drinking waters were brought out in buckets.9 Mail was sporadic. Medicine was scarce or none at all. Haircuts were provided by the Japanese Americans. The prisoners were beaten needlessly. Japanese families traditionally require daily hot baths or showers, but they were infrequently provided and many times the water came in a bucket, cold. Soap and shampoo were a luxury.

Photo 17. An inside look at the U.S built concentration hut: note the uninsulated walls with no windows and no running water, sinks, mirrors, restrooms with privacy, or stoves. In addition, there were no washing machines or dryers, nor did they have any furnace for warm air for the Winter months. How would you like to live under those conditions for three years?

A. The Family Unit:

About 60% of Japanese homes are owner occupied and approximately 34 % are leased by the private sector, and the remainder are owned by companies or local government for their workers.[24] The Japanese generally will not invite you to their home because of the smallness of their dwelling. Inviting you to a restaurant is more traditional.[24]

Photo 18. The Japanese dinner eaten with chopsticks; this is also true for the breakfast and lunch.

The Japanese family (*Kazoku*) is a foundational part of the Japanese society. An individual's identity, reputation, obligations, and responsibilities are deeply connected to their family. Japanese family structures have been influenced by Confucian ideas of filial piety and defined hierarchical social relationships over the centuries. The traditional family unit in Japan consists of a mother, father, and their children. Traditionally, three-generation households are the norm although this is changing with time—with adult children living with their parents and their own husband and kids.[7]

B. The Japanese Immigrant Culture:

What is important to the Japanese culture is a mix of old and new beliefs, traditions, and customs. There is an art, reason, and historical purpose to explain how things are conducted in families and in society— making the Japanese culture unique. From tea ceremonies to flower arranging, these customs will give you a taste of Japanese traditions. Flower arranging or *Ikebana*, is more than just the arrangement of flowers. The Japanese people viewed it as an important religious art form. The most important Japanese cultural and family traditions revolved around working together and living in peace. One of the old traditions is *Sushi*, which is especially eaten during religious holidays. Some of the predominant values in the Japanese culture include:

Harmony

Politeness

Respect

Formality

Photo 19. An assortment of sushi; raw fish (Sashimi) with sushi is a favorite for the Japanese-American culture.

Family roles—the members of the family take their work and school very seriously. Their schools and colleges are very competitive and they must study endlessly and compete tirelessly to get into the universities —many times their children commit suicide because of the pressures and entrance-exam failures.

Formalities are important in the Japanese Culture. How you address others is a sign of respect and reverence. This is evident through the body language and speech.[7]

Greeting someone with a bow is comparable to shaking someone's hand in the U.S.

The *eshaku* is a semi-formal bow used for greeting and meeting new people. It involves bowing at a 15-degree angle.

The *saikeirei* bow is a 45-degree angle bow used for showing the highest form of respect.

In terms of language, Japanese people address individuals according to age, gender, and relationship, where older people and customers require more formal speech.

Unless you have a casual relationship (i.e., Between friends or with a child), adhere to appropriate formal titles by using *"-san"* or *"-sama"* after a person's last name.

The mother in the family is responsible for cooking the meals, taking care of the children, shopping for the family groceries, cleaning the home spotless, and helping the children do the homework. While the head of the household brings the bread home, the other half is responsible for paying the bills. Unlike the Chinese male, she is responsible for caring for their parents.

The husband or father is the patriarch of the household. He is responsible for the family's household income, the family's wellbeing and health, economic stability, scholarly activities. All decisions are determined by the patriarch of the household.

The Japanese take great pride in the preparation and consumption of their foods. They have strict public dining etiquette.[7, 24] It is customary to remove your shoes and sit on the *tatami* or straw floor. In addition:

It is traditional to wait until all parties have received their order in the restaurant or the husband is served first before the rest of the family before eating.

You'll often hear Japanese people saying *"itadakimasu"* a polite way of showing appreciation as you receive the meal and *"gochigochisosama deshita"* as a thank you once you have finished eating.

When drinking liquor like *sake*, a strong rice wine (About 15- 18% alcohol), it is considered polite to fill a friend's glass with liquor before yours. Today, beer has now overtaken sake as the most popular drink with meals.

While finishing every last grain of rice and noisily slurping your soup is not considered rude, but it's a sign you're enjoying your food.

You should lift the rice bowl with your left hand to your mouth to eat more efficiently. The soup bowl should be drunk directly from the bowl. Rice (Gohan) is a Japanese staple and is the major ingredient of the meal. Using the Japanese style toilet requires the squatting position. For most Westerners this isn't that comfortable, but it is hygienic.

To the Japanese, the traditional tea ceremony is an important cultural and ritual art form, which takes a host or hostess years to master. Steeped in Zen Buddhism, it focuses on living in the moment. A formal tea ceremony last about two-four hours. Guests must wash their hands and mouth with water before entering the tea room to symbolize purification.

Don't try to make routine eye contact; like so much else in Japan the direct approach is avoided.

Meishi: exchanging business cards—shaking hands and bowing first before a slight bow and handing your card (The right side up so it can be read immediately).

Photo 20. A Japanese traditional tea ceremony, which follows a ritual and spiritual format.

C. Role of Buddhist Religion:

Photo 21. The Japanese immigrants living in America are primarily Shinto and Buddhist.

Shinto and Buddhism are the two main religions in Japan.[7] The Japanese immigrants in America are predominantly Buddhist, while the Japanese Americans are a mixture of different Protestants. Religion in Japan is viewed as more of a moral code than a doctrine that is preached. It is a way of life for most Japanese people that is not separate from their social and cultural values. In Japan there is a complete separation of religion and state, which makes religious practices private, family affairs. In Shintoism involves the belief that every living thing found in nature contain Gods or *kami*. Buddhism is more concerned with the soul and the afterlife.

D.   Role of Education:

Photo 22. A 3-year-old Japanese girl is starting preschool early to prepare for the rigorous grade-school, junior-high, high-school, and college. Private universities are even more difficult to pass the entrance examinations.

The Japanese School System primarily consist of:

Six-years of elementary school

Three-year of junior-high school

Three-year of high school

Followed by two- to three-year junior college

Or four-year college or university

The Japanese family take education very seriously. Once in the college or university, they are expected to graduate because of the intense preparation. Some of the more well-to-do families do whatever is possible to get their children into private universities. The Japanese college students are committed to finish college to *"not lose face to the parents and community."* It is not uncommon that the college ungraduated commits suicide if they do not complete the private college or university.

Latest statistics show that 19% of the American population have at least a Bachelor's degree and 11% have a postgraduate degree; while 30% of Asians have at least a Bachelor's degree and 21% have a postgraduate degree. During 2010, the percentage that graduated with a Bachelor's Degree or higher by race:[7]

Asian Americans	50%
White Americans	31%
Black Americans	18%
Pacific Islander Americans	15%
Hispanic Americans	13%

It is yet unclear that the education level has a direct effect on discrimination and racism practices. There is some evidence that having higher education might have contributed to racism in the work place. There appears to be other more powerful influences such as:

The appearance of the ethnic groups

The parental upbringing

Violent gangs in the streets

History of crimes in the city

Availability of illegal guns

Jealously and envy of a given culture

Different facial looks and physical attributes

Role of religion in the upbringing

E. The Effects of the War:

When the Japanese surprise attack on Pearl Harbor occurred on December 7, 1941; the losses were great:[7]

2,403 American-service members

1,143 wounded

8 battleships

30 destroyers

5 submarines destroyed

3 US Coast Guard cutters destroyed

390 US aircraft destroyed

6 aircraft carriers destroyed

103 civilians killed or wounded

1 Army aircraft shot down

3 one-man submarines

This war inflamed the American public; all the good that the Japanese Americans did was totally erased. The racism and discrimination were so bad that the Chinese Americans had to wear painted signs, *"I'm Chinese"* to protect themselves from the hate crimes that were being inflicted on Japanese Americans.

Photo 23. Japanese dive bombers on their Way to Kaneohe Naval station which is located on the opposite side of Pearl Harbor.

Photo 24. The bombing of U.S. Navy ships at Kaneohe Bay by Japanese dive bombers.

The gates to North America were now closed to the Japanese immigrants, but the struggle for Japanese exclusion into the United States did not end; it merely diverted southward into South America. From 1908 to 1941, 190,000 Japanese immigrants entered Brazil and 20,000 entered Peru.[7] As the population of immigrants grew in Latin America, so did the anti-Japanese sentiment and hostilities. Brazil soon implemented a law similar to the 1924 United States' Immigration Act to set quotas for Japanese Americans entering Brazil (2,711). Peru followed with a quota of 16,000. The widespread banning of Japanese immigration in North and South America was an epidemic.[7]

Racism continued after WW II ended with the Japanese Americans. There were numerous signs posted throughout the United States: *"Japs Go Home", "You're Not Wanted—Leave America", "We Hate Japs"*. This is another example of *"rights gone wrong.*[9]*"* None were posted in Hawaii.

Photo 25. Japs move on. This is a White neighborhood; this was the height of cruelty and racism in America.

I have a best friend, Timothy Marutani, a 3rd generation Japanese American like me (*Sansei*), who unlike me, experienced racism in Texas in every way by possible by a White person. I, on the other hand, did not experience discrimination while growing up and going to school in Hawaii.

To survive these hate crimes, one first needs to understand the cultural mentality of the Japanese American people— *"Don't Rock the Boat to assimilate into the American mainstream culture"*. There were some Japanese Americans that stood at the forefront of Justice. Tim's uncle, the honorable William Marutani, fought for justice. For example, he was one of the many the mixed marriages couples that were banned throughout America.

Photo 26. This Black and Asian American were the best of friends. They are colorblind; they have been ever since high school.

Photo: 27. Mixed Marriages in America; White American and Japanese American marriages were starting to pick in the late 1900s.

Judge William Marutani, who handled the cases, gave Asian Americans a voice a pivotal moment in constitutional history. Only about 1700 people of Japanese descent lived in Virginia as of 1960 according to the U.S. census, but the Japanese American Citizens League (JCLA), which had fought for years against interracial-marriage bans throughout America, wanted to show how Virgin's law hurt even small minority groups. William Marutani argued in court that the state of Virginia prohibited only White people from marrying their race, thus allowing all other races to intermarry, exposing the ban for "exactly what it is—a White Supremacy Law[6, 8]" He also said, "I think Martin Luther King put it very succinctly—He said 'injustice anywhere is a threat to justice everywhere' and that is true."

The number of race-based hate crime victims in the United States in 2020 were as follows; note Asians Americans were not at the top of the list:

Anti-Black	2,884
Anti-Jewish	1,109
Anti-White	875
Anti-Hispanic	557
Anti-Hispanic	517
Anti-Other	298
Anti-Asian/Pacific Islander	281
Anti-Physical	20
Anti-Mental	16

There were 246,900 hate crimes reported in 2020 in the USA; but who were the perpetrators?

1. White Supremist
2. Black Americans
3. Hispanic Americans
4. Religion (Anti-Semitism)

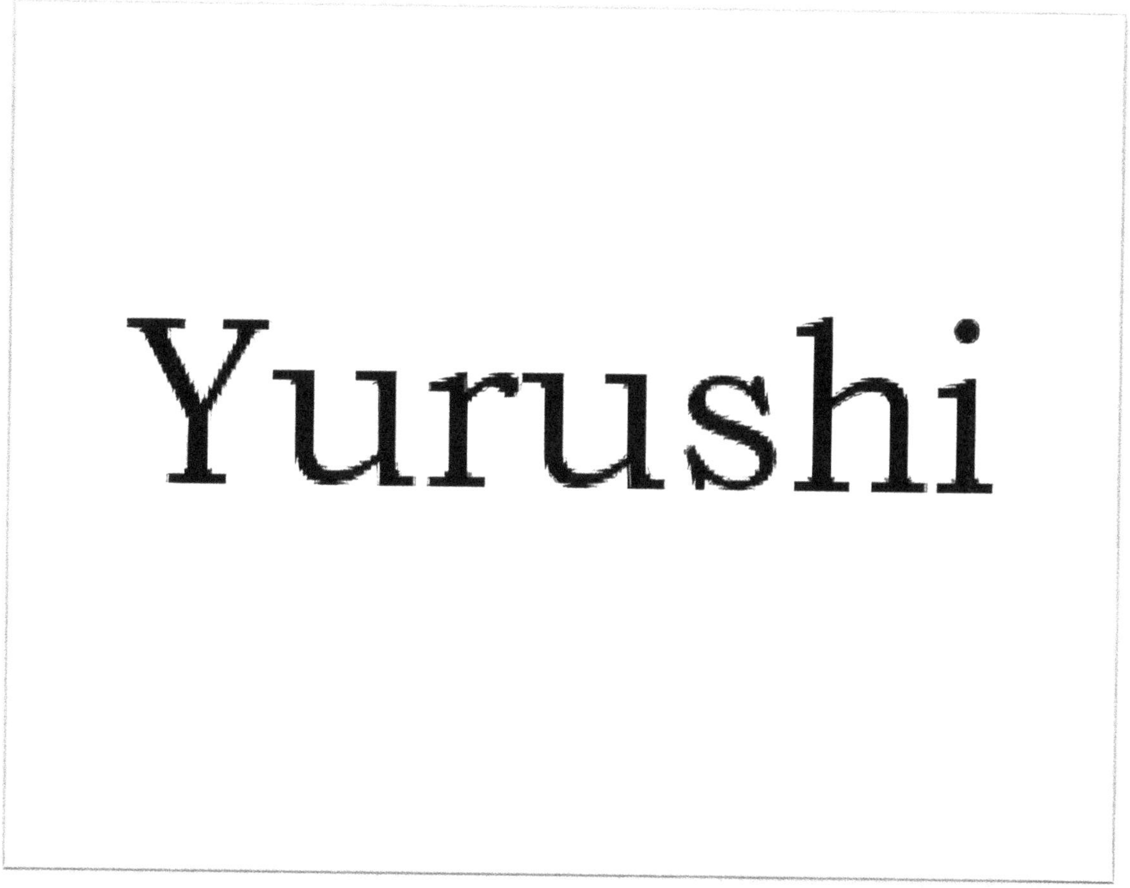

Yurushi

Figure 3. *Japanese word that translates to Forgiveness.*[17]

Chapter 5
Arrival of The Korean Immigrants

The high unemployment rate, political insecurity, and military dictatorship caused massive numbers of South Koreans to immigrate to the United States in the 1960s through the 1980s. Their children, known as the 2nd generation (Known as *gyopo*) compose as the present-day Korean-American community. The United States has the largest South Korean immigrant population in the world. The South Korean immigrants were that last group of Asians to enter the United States of America. They located mostly in California (345,882), New York (119, 846), New Jersey (65,349), Illinois (51,453), Washington (46,279), Texas (45,571), Virginia (45,279), Maryland (39,155), Pennsylvania (35,612), Georgia, (28,945), and Hawaii (23,537). A third of the Korean immigrants became merchants like the businesses in Korean Town in Los Angeles. The 100 Korean immigrants that arrived in Honolulu during 1903, worked in the sugar cane and pineapple fields. During the next two years, more than 7,000 Koreans arrived in Hawaii, recruited by as strikebreakers by the Hawaiian planters. However, this predominant channel of avenue of work was closed in 1905, when the Japanese government, concerned about the welfare of Japanese workers in Hawaii, successfully pressured the Korean government to halt the emigration to Hawaii. The passage of the *1926 Asian Exclusion Act* closed the doors from the U.S. side. The lack of interest and aptitude of the first wave of Koreans in these types of work fled the fields—more than any other ethnic group.

Between 2004 and 2010, South Korea enacted a series of sweeping immigration and citizenship reforms that opened its borders to unskilled immigration, extended local voting rights to permanent foreign residents, and allowed people to hold dual nationality. South Korea was the first country in Asia to grant permanent foreign residents local voting rights—something not even Western countries with reputations for more liberal immigration and citizenship policies such as France and Germany have done. The South Korean government also invested heavily in social integration programs. After the promulgation of the Support for *Multicultural Families Act in 2008*, the budget for programs to support immigrant spouses and what are termed multicultural families increased from $28 million to $498 million in 2020. These reforms did not stop the South-Koreans from going to the United States. In 2017, approximately 1 million South Koreans immigrants resided in the United States—representing 2.4% of the 44.5 million immigrants in this country. After the *Immigration Act of 1965* removed restrictions on Asian Immigration to America, The Korean immigrant population grew significantly—from 11,000 in 1960 to 290,000 in 1980[10].

The contemporary Korean immigrants tend to be highly educated and of high-socioeconomic standing compared to other immigrant groups and overall U.S. populations. South Korean students have consistently been among the top three largest groups of international students enrolled U.S. higher-education institutions along with Chinese and Indian nationals.

Most Korean immigrants in America are naturalized citizens, and those who have gained lawful permanent resident also known as green-card holders have relied on sponsorship from their employer or immediate relative. Overall, compared to the total foreign-born population, Korean immigrants have higher incomes and educational attainment and are less likely to experience poverty or lack health- insurance policies.

In 1905, Mary Lee's family was driven out of their home by Japanese soldiers who had taken control of Korea.[7] They walked for several days and nights until they reached the port city of Inchon, Korea. There, they saw two ships with men ready to recruit Korean laborers to work on the Hawaiian plantations. They were a minority. Because 90% of the Korean immigrants that emigrated to the U.S. were male laborers, there were a lot of inter-racial marriages in both Hawaii and on the mainland. Several hundred settled in central California to farm in agriculture and became prosperous businessmen.

The 2nd wave of immigration occurred in the decade following the Korean War and was dominated by students who came to America for graduate education.

The 3rd wave of Korean immigration to the United States was made possible by the *1965 Hart-Celler Act*, which greatly liberalized the *National Origin Quota System* and opened the door to largely expanded immigration from non-European countries, including South Korea. The 3rd wave of immigration differed significantly from the first two— namely that immigrants were often college-educated and brought families with them when they immigrated, which make them the majority living in America today. There are many Korean Americans that made their mark in the United States. For example, Angela E. Oh is an attorney, teacher, and public lecturer known for speaking against discrimination and harassment of minority groups. Ms. Oh famously gained national prominence as a spokesperson and mediator for Asian American community following the Los Angeles riots. In 1997, she was appointed by President Bill Clinton to the *President's Initiative on Race*. She served as part of a seven-member Advisory Board in an effort directed at examining how race, racism, and racial differences have affected the United States. There are others such as Nora Lum, a famous comedian actress, Chloe Kim who won a gold medal for snowboarding at the 2018 Winter Olympic Games at the age of 17 (Youngest ever), Roy Choi is a famous chef who gained prominence as the creator of the gourmet Korean- Mexican taco. In 1905, Yongman Park came to the U.S. to study at the University of Nebraska. While studying there he established the Korean Youth Military Academy and wrote two books: "The National Military" (1911) and "Soldiers Requisite Knowledge" (1912). Syngman Rhee came to the United States in 1904 to study and receive his PhD in International Affairs from Princeton University in 1910. He returned to South Korea and became the first president in 1948. There were many other countless celebrities and scholars that immigrated to America to make their mark. But life in America was messy.[12]

Life was not all 'sugar and cream' with the Korean immigrants living in America. According to a survey conducted by the National Human Rights Commission of Korea among foreign residents in South Korea in 2019, 68.4% of the respondents declared they experienced racial discrimination, mainly due to their Korean language spoken in public.[7] The 2018 interview with Gi-Wook Shin with the Asia Experts Forum, suggests that Korea is very homogeneous; only about 5% of the population is non-ethnic Korean. South Korea is trying to promote Korean culture around the world and is fairly new and popular; they are proud of that development.

Korean Americans have emerged as one of the most misunderstood ethnic groups in America. The image of Korean American merchants defending their stores with guns sent shock waves throughout the Country. The Korean Americans were often stereotyped as being rude, disrespectful, and greedy. Korean Americans merchants in several cities were accused of exploiting and oppressing the African American communities in which their stores were located, and African American leaders often led boycotts of their stores. The distorted images and stereotypes were constantly projected and reinforced by the media. Merchant-customer disputes were made into race wars by the newspaper and television and radio news media. Black American rap singer retaliated by channeling their anger and frustration in anti-Korean songs.

Anti-Asian crimes rise despite progress with civil-right laws$_3$ Mass shootings came amid a historic increase in violence Asian Americans during the corona virus-19 pandemic. Since then, the federal government has passed more legislation to combat hate crimes and a Georgia prosecutor announced that she is seeking the death penalty for the 22-year-old White Atlanta gunman for four of the killings—a sentence made possible by the state's new hate crimes statute. The suspect pleaded guilty to the four murders and was sentenced to life in prison. All of this amid a White man who killed eight massage therapists, six of them Korean American women at three spas in the Atlanta area—as clear acts of racism. Experts on hate crimes told USA Today the charges acknowledged the traumatic impact the shootings had on the victims, their friends and families and the Asian-American community. Hate crimes are rarely federally prosecuted, although there have been increased efforts to track such crimes, lawmakers need to do more to prevent the violence and make the community feel safe. Prevention is key. This is a national problem that we cannot arrest or enforce our way out of according to Michael Lieberman, senior policy counsel for hate and extremism at the Southern Poverty Law Center. Attacks against women of Asian descent—including the subway killing of Michelle Go, who was fatally shoved from behind in front a New York subway car by a homeless man on Jan 20, 2022. Despite the fact that the Asian - American community is reeling from the hate crime, the NY police is not investigating the crime. Ms. Go was described by friends as beautiful, brilliant, kind, and educated woman who loved her family and friends, loved to travel the world to help others. On February 1, 2022, Christina Yuna Lee, a Korean-American graduate of Rutgers University was brutally stabbed to death in her Chinatown apartment. It's the latest in a spate of attacks against the Asian population that have accelerated since the start of the coronavirus pandemic, first detected in Wuhan, China. Ms. Lee was a 35-year-old Korean woman who was stabbed 40 times by a homeless man who followed her inside her building. The NY police said the alleged killer, Assamad Nash, was charged with murder and burglary.

There is very little research on what strategies can effectively prevent prejudiced crimes because the motivating factors are so complex and it's difficult to predict who might commit these kind of hate crimes. Most offenders are young White men who have little criminal history and do not know their victims and are part of an organized hate group, according to Phillis Gerstenfeld, a California State University professor who studies hate crimes. She said that education and improved messaging around tolerance is the best way to prevent violence. Uncovering the root causes of the problem are required to make an impact on reducing this issue. A University of Akron (Ohio) professor, Dr. Toni Bisconti, who researches discrimination and diversity-related education, said the burden of educating others shouldn't fall [on] to minority communities. She said, increasing access to mental health resources in schools could help identify students who have problems before hate escalates into violence. She also makes the comment that "one of the biggest problems with grade school and junior high and even high school education is we don't teach basic anger management or conflict management." As state lawmakers and school boards attempt to restrict what lessons about race and history can be taught, ethnic studies programs have the greatest promise for addressing the root cause of social conditioning. Cynthia Choi, co-executive director of Stop AAPI Hate (A nonprofit that was formed to track violence and negative rhetoric aimed at Asian Americans) said that increased investment in community-based solutions is critical because of the traumatic effect incidents have had on Asian Americans and Pacific Islanders.

A. The Family Unit:

Photo 28. A young Korean girl is eating dinner with a spoon, unlike the Chinese or Japanese cultures who use chopsticks.

Traditionally, the typical family type in Korea was a patrilocal- stem family. The stem family generally consists of two families in successive generation, a father and mother living in the same household with the married oldest son, his wife, and their children. The eldest son usually inherited the family estate.[31]

Photo 29. A young Korean-American girl wearing her traditional formal dress.

American parents strongly believe, unlike the Korean Americans, that their children should not cling on to their parents, but rather be independent. In addition, American parents believe that their children will not support them when they get old and do not expect to live with their children. Most Korean Americans find this bewildering and inhuman. The close family ties and dependencies are valued so highly in the Korean culture that it is unthinkable to abandon these customs. To Koreans such autonomy is not a virtue— "a life in which egos are all autonomous, separate discrete, and self-sufficient is too cold, impersonal, lonely, and inhuman.

Children incur debt to their parents who gave birth to them and raised them is a filial duty. It is understood that the children must treat their parents respectfully at all times, take care of them in their old age, mourn for them at their funeral, and perform ceremonies for them after their death, which is not enough— to act responsibly by paying all their financial debts.[31]

One thing you should obey is their long tradition of keeping their home clean. The Korean Americans, like the Japanese Americans still do *NOT* wear their shoes into their spotless house. Always take your shoes off outside and place the pair neatly on the side. Unlike the Japanese Americans, the Koreans prefer that you wear socks indoors because they entertain on the floor, play with their children on the floor, and eat on the floor on a low table because they sit on the floor on a straw mat.[10] For that reason, they expect their floors to be immaculate.

Photo 30. The Korean American household still lives by the traditional way of entering their home with just socks and not with shoes.

More than Japanese and Chinese, Koreans adhere to traditional Confucian principles of family organization. Confucius and his followers taught that only a Country where family life was harmonious could be peaceful and prosperous.

According to James Hoare[10], the Chinese long ago described the Korean people as the Eastern country of courteous people. This aphorism reflected the Koreans' traditional esteem for decorum, courtesy, and propriety, derived from the teachings of Confucian. The Koreans do not favor demonstrative behavior in front of those they do not know well. They tend to be remote and may seem stand-offish in the presence of strangers. They are not necessarily friendly toward people they meet on the street. On the whole Koreans do not feel obliged to greet in a friendly fashion those whom they have not been introduced. One aspect of traditional Korea that has survived is widespread respect for those who are older. You may find that Korean young people are reluctant to eat, drink alcohol, or smoke in front of parents or teachers. If you are young, you may find that an older Korean will abandon you in mid-conversation to talk to an older colleague. Confucius emphasized respect for the elderly, but he meant elderly men. Neither women nor children ranked very high in his priority system. There are family taboos, like the use of the left hand to offer an object to someone. To use the left hand is seen by all Koreans as offensive especially if they are elderly. Do not stick chopsticks upright in rice, as this resembles the way incense is burned at funerals. Bare feet are generally to be avoid. Koreans live, eat, and sleep on the floor, so it is important that floors are spotlessly clean. Not wearing socks mean that your feet will be dirty. Do not touch an adult on the head, or even on the shoulder. This same prohibition does not apply to children or youngsters. Unlike the Japanese and the Chinese, Koreans use a spoon instead of chopsticks. Sometimes you will be given wooden chopsticks in a restaurant. The most famous of all Korean side dish is **kimchi**. It is a pickled cabbage seasoned with red pepper, ginger and LOTS of garlic—you will smell like garlic for miles and miles for days and days! Don't ever underestimate the spiciness of the kimchi because it can be darn *HOT*. During my interviews with Korean Americans, I've been informed that their temperament can be *short fused* and *hot tempered* that matches the hotness of the kimchi.

When drinking, you should NEVER pour your own drink first. You should hold your glass in front of you with both hands or with the right hand supported under the elbow by the left hand. When you go to a restaurant, don't go Dutch; Koreans will customarily pay the entire bill. So, don't be cheap. Koreans do not generally hug each other or kiss on the check when greeting one another. A bow or a handshake with a weak grip will be sufficient.

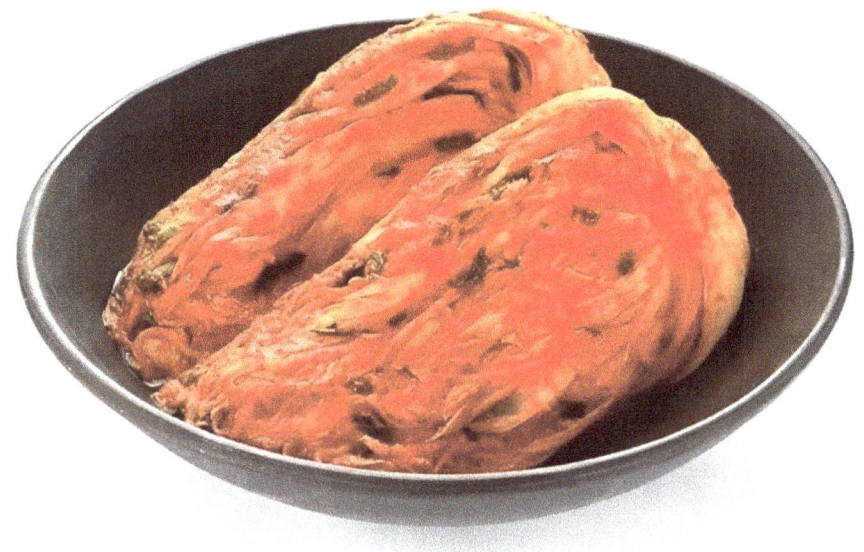

Photo 31. One of the most popular and traditional cultural foods is Kimchi; It is made of different types of cabbages or cucumbers with lots of garlic and hot spicy peppers[15].

B. The Korean Immigrant Culture:

What is the Korean Culture like? It includes traditions like the ethical code of conduct in social life and showing respect to the elders and family. The Koreans also believe in sincerity and loyalty, and follow certain codes of conduct while meeting, eating, praying, and even when celebrating. When many other cultures would shake hands, Koreans bow. Korean Americans tend to display a strong respect for educated people and emphasize their children's education as one of the highest responsibilities in life. The Korean culture is unique because of their mindset of diligent and hard work, filial piety, humbleness, and their economic success during their short stay in America[10].

Korean Americans are very family-orientated. The family are very loyal to each other and dedicated to maintaining their characteristic of collectivist societies. By placing family harmony over individual happiness, many Koreans emphasize the importance of family, rather than self-expression. Korean values and customs established under Confucianism include the following:

Authority of fathers

Wives' obedience to husbands

Children's obedience to parents

Filial piety submission of self to family

Submission to civil authorities

High expectations in education

Of all the groups of immigrants coming to the USA each year, Koreans are said to be among the most successful—many reaching the highest levels of achievement in this Country in a single generation. Many Korean immigrants settled in Los Angeles and in New York and went into business; nearly half opened their own business—like Korean import shops, green grocers, dry cleaning, finger nail salons. The language barrier prevented many Korean immigrants from getting decent jobs. Without that strong network of Koreans that helped each other, it has been much, much more difficult not only to gain access to an opportunity to make money, but also an opportunity to get capital to start a business. Koreans supported each other by pooling money to provide no-interest loans to help the newest immigrants start their businesses. The national trend has moved away from independently owned business altogether. The East of Eden Grocery store on 79th and York Avenue is now a Chase Bank owned by Korean Americans. The Korean population have a unique business model that they follow— called *keh*. This creative financial technique adapted from their homeland to help launch one of the most spectacular growths in small business creation of any American ethnic group in this century. Keh is a club in which Korean members contribute money each month, then wait for their turn to the recipient of the group pot of money.

C. The Role of Buddhism, Confucianism, & Christianity:

Families were very different among the three historical periods Shilla Dynasty (57 B.C.E.-C.E. 935), Koryo Dynasty (C.E.918-1392), and Chosum Dynasty (C.E. 1392-1910) because of their religious orientation.

Buddhism was introduced in Korea during the Early Kingdoms (C.E. 372), and was adopted as the state religion for a millennium.

Photo 32. Elaborate Confucius Church

Its emphasis was on rejecting worldly values and concerns, including the family. However, Buddhism delivered a message contrary to that of Confucianism. Buddhism's influence was limited to the sphere of individual self-enlightenment and discipline, and it appealed principally to the ruling class because the majority of the people who lived at a subsistence level had few material possessions to renounce. As a result, relatively few people were affected by the self-abnegation and anti-familial monasticism that Buddhism taught. The religion's influence declined further during the late Koryo Dynasty when Buddhist groups in Korea became corrupt. They constructed extravagant temples, and followers of the religion observed on superficial rituals. When the Chosun Dynasty succeeded the Koryo Dynasty in 1392, it adopted Confucianism as the familial and state philosophy, suppressing Buddhism. The term Confucianism is used to refer the popular value system of China, Korea, and Japan. This system was derived from the synthesis of the traditional cultural values espoused by Confucius and his followers and subsequently by elements of Taoism, Legalism, and Mohism.

Confucianism declared the family the fundamental unit of society, responsible for economic functions of production and consumption, as well as education and socialization—guided by moral and ethical principles. In its teachings, Confucianism has traditionally deified ancestors, institutionalized ancestor worship, and delegated the duties of master to the head of the male lineage—that is to the father and husband. Confucianism is a familial religion; as it took hold, the ideal of male superiority within the patrilineal family became more prominent in the Chosum Dynasty.

The family is the basic component of social life in Korea, and its perpetuation has been of paramount importance under patriarchal Confucianism. In a Confucian patriarchal family, the family as an entity takes precedence over its individual members, and the family group is inseparably identified with the clan. The most function of the family members is to maintain and preserve the household within the traditional Confucian system. Society became organized around principles—males shall dominate the females and that the elder shall dominate the young.

The aged (Both males and females) were highly respected and the women were often self-assertive and highly valued and were delegated the responsibility of maintaining the family finance. Once in the United States, the Korean Americans began to switch religion; many changed to Protestant and Methodist religions. This had an impact on their attitudes, thinking, and conduct. Inpatients is common in the Korean culture<i>3</i>[1]. That's why everyone crowds around the bus door, vying to go in first, instead of forming a line. Sometimes on the street, hurried Koreans will bump you without apology and hurry away.

D. The Role of Education:

Photo 33. Korean-American students at college for higher education for greater economic success.

Chapter 6
ASIAN-AMERICAN CASE STUDIES

Case-Study 1

How the Tree of Life Killings affect Hate Crimes

Before I start with Asian-American case studies, I asked what can we learn from other races and cultures on prejudices and hate crimes? I would like to start with the American Jews and their religion's effect on racism.

The Tree of Life killings occurred in a Pittsburgh L'Simcha Congregation on October 27, 2018 with 11 deaths. The antisemitic killings of 11 American Jews by a White supremist using a Colt AR- 15SP1 semiautomatic rifle and three Glock .357 SIG handguns. The lone suspect, 46year-old Robert Gregory Bowers had earlier posted antisemitic comments against HIAS (Hebrew Immigrant Aid Society) online. His parents were divorced when he was one-year old. His father died by suicide when he was seven-year-old. His mother married a Florida man when he was a toddler and lived with them until they separated a year after their marriage. At the age of 26, Robert was charged with rape. He lived with his mother's parents and attended Baldwin High School but never finished. He worked as a trucker and was deeply involved with posting anti-Semitic conspiracy theories on Gab, a social media website that promoted neo-Nazis, White supremacist's theories.

The religion is a Conservative Jewish Congregation in the Squirrel Hill area of Pittsburgh where there were typically low in crimes. The Squirrel Hill neighborhood is one of the largest predominantly Jewish American neighborhoods in the United States and has historically been the center of Pittsburgh's Jewish community. About 26% of the city's Jewish population live in the area.

Photo 34. Orthodox Jewish People

So, what is the root-cause of all this hate?

Is it based on religion?

Is it based on Race?

Is it based on ethnicity?

Is it based on color?

Is it based on their looks, especially if they looked like Orthodox Jews?

Is it based on ancestry and their traditions?

In 2018 and 2019, reports of anti-Semitism in the United States were reported to have increased compared to previous years according to the FBI. Anti-Semitism in America has existed for centuries; most Jewish community relations agencies draw distinctions between anti-Semitism, which is measured in terms of attitudes and behaviors, and the security and status of American Jews. Both measured by the occurrence of specific incidents. The FBI data show that 7,314 hate crimes during 2018 —the highest number since 2008. Hate crimes based on race ethnicity, religion, or ancestry continue to be the area of biggest concern across the United States. Anti-Black hate crimes continue to be the largest single category of incidents with 1,930 in 2019, a number that has held relatively steady for the past three years. Anti-Hispanic or Latino incidents are becoming an increasing concern, with 527 total incidents, an increase of 9% since 2018 and 23% since 2007. The other largest categories of hate crimes include anti-gay incidents with 746 and anti-White incidents with a total of 666.

Case-Study 2

Rape of Nanking Massacre

This documentary was written by Iris Chang[4], a Chinese American. It is about the atrocities and the cruelty committed by the Japanese Imperial army when they attacked Nanking, China during 1937. They burned the city down, butchered an estimated 200,000 to 300,000 male war prisoners, massacred and additional 50,000 civilians, and raped at lease 20,000-80,000 women and children of all ages. Racism against the Chinese was the probable cause.

A small group of Western businessmen and missionaries, the *International Committee for Nanking Safety Zone*, attempted to set up a neutral area of the city that would provide refuge for Nanking's citizens. Though the Japanese solders initially agreed to respect the *Nanking Safety Zone*, ultimately not even these refugees were safe from the vicious attacks.

Entire families were massacred, and even the elderly and infants were targeted for execution, tens of thousands of women and children were raped. Some of the solders inserted objects into the children's vagina to see how large or wide an object they could accommodate.

General Matsui Iwane and his Lieutenant Tani Hisao were tried and convicted for war crimes by the International Military Tribunal for the Far East and were executed. Anger over the events at Nanking continues to color Sino-Japanese relations to this day.

Iris Chang lived in California and made several trips to Nanking, China to directly interview the victims like an Investigative Reporter. Over time the stress of the interviews took a toll; she started to lose weight and clumps of hair started to come off when she brushed her hair. Her parents repeatedly pleaded with Iris to stop writing the book. She said, "She had a mission to uncover the truth by publishing the book." On November 9, 2004 she was found in her car on a rural road south of Los Gatos, dead from an apparently self-inflicted gunshot wound. How sad.

Such atrocities could be done by mankind and affect mankind[4]. Evil does exist and still prevails!

Over 80 years bitterness still persists between two countries— Japan and Korea, whereby sex slavery, forced prostitution, and other abuses occurred. According to historical records, petitions from survivors from China, Philippines, Indonesia, Australia, and East Timor were sent to the U.N.'s International Court of Justice last week to file human-rights complaints.

Photo 35. Japanese Imperial soldiers attacked China, including Nanking, China, looted the cities, murdered Chinese soldiers and people and raped women and children (3-to 80-years old).

Case-Study 3

The Transcontinental Railroad Chinese Laborers:

From 1863 to 1869, roughly 15,000-20,000 Chinese immigrants helped build the transcontinental railroad across the United States. They toiled through back-breaking labor during both frigid winters and blazing-hot summers. They were paid less than the White American workers and they lived in poorer conditions (In non-heated tents) while the White workers were given accommodations in train cars. Like their fellow Chinese immigrants who came to California for the gold rush and then on to Idaho, railroad workers were treated harshly and cruelly. The Chinese were butchered like hogs to steal their gold nuggets.

The Chinese immigrants helped achieve one of the greatest engineering feats in U.S. history, but their sacrifices are seldom remembered. The railroad was built largely by Chinese and Irish immigrants plus the Mormon laborers, but it laid the foundation for deepening racial tension that are still felt today. This year, it comes at a time of increasing anti-Asian hate crimes worldwide amid and ongoing Covid-19 pandemic that disproportionately affects communities of color. The roots of anti-Asian racism across America stretch back over 100 years. Understanding this hate crime can help uncover some of today's violence, which is critical factor to building a healthier new future.

For as long as Asians have been in the United States, they have been labelled as outsiders who can't be trusted, and that misperception has often led to tragic consequence[29].

The Union Pacific Railroad began laying railroad tracks near Omaha, Nebraska and the Central Pacific Railroad Company started in Sacramento, California. The two railroad companies met a Promontory Summit, Utah—completing the first Transcontinental Railroad on May 10, 1869. The railroad was completed in the end of 1969. It was primarily the Chinese immigrants who did this backbreaking work--while being denied the ability to become American citizens!

The laborers slaved 10-12 hours shifts during six-day work weeks. Many of the Chinese immigrants froze in their shoes and fell to the ground and left there until the Spring thaw when the bones were gathered to be sent home to China.

The *Page Act of 1875*, one of the earliest pieces of federal legislation that restricted immigration from East Asia—stopped almost all Chinese women from entering the Country, stereotyping them as prostitutes. Then came the *Chinese Exclusion Act of 1882*— which barred anyone from China, and it also declared Chinese Immigrants ineligible for naturalization. This law made it nearly impossible for Chinese families to set roots in the United States. One of the largest mass lynchings in the U.S. history targeted Chinese immigrants. For over a century, Chinese workers' contributions were obscured and diminished. Remembering these Chinese workers isn't important only to Asian American history, it is vital to American history[28, 29].

Case-Study 4

The Chinese Exclusion Act and Human Trafficking, Prostitution, and Slave Labor:

The Chinese Exclusion Act was a U.S. federal law signed by President Chester A. Arthur on May 6, 1882—prohibiting all immigration of Chinese laborers into the United States for 10 years. The reason this law was enacted because many Whites feared that the Chinese immigrants would end up taking their jobs. This law was repealed by the *1943 Magnuson Act* when China had become an ally of the U.S. against Japan in World War II, as the Americans needed to embody and image of fairness and justice. If any Chinese were caught entering America, they were fined $500, which was a lot back then. White Americans who caught any Chinese entering the Country made them sign a contract to work as a prostitute—today known as Human Trafficking.

The 1982 law affected the Chinese immigrants who were already living in the United States by prohibiting the Chinese immigrants from becoming American citizens.

President Donald Trump said, "minority workers have been among those hit the hardest by unfettered immigration." But there is a racially charged history to the idea that immigrant workers depress American wages, an argument that led to the Country's first immigration restriction law in 1882. Donald Trump also started dismantling the Diversity Visa Lottery Program—known as the *Green Card Lottery*. This program is administered by the Department of State as a way to increase the diversity of the immigrants coming to live in America. Each year, the program allows 50,000 randomly selected people by a computer (Only from countries that don't send many immigrants to the United States) to obtain permanent residency. It is a way for individuals and families who otherwise wouldn't have any way to legally immigrate to America to get a *Green Card*. For the 2023 application period, nationals from the following countries were NOT eligible to apply:

Bangladesh

Brazil

Canada

China

Columbia

Dominican Republic

El Salvador

Haiti

Honduras

Hong Kong

India

Jamaica

Mexico

Nigeria

Pakistan

Philippines

South Korea

United Kingdom (Except Northern Ireland)

Venezuela

Vietnam

If your native country is not eligible, there are still two ways you could qualify for the *Green Card*:

If your spouse was born in an eligible country, you can apply with your spouse and choose your spouse's birth country on your application. If neither of your parents were legal residents in your own country of birth, you can choose your mother's or father's country of birth. Cheap Chinese slaves filled every of the job market and they were called "Chinese *coolie*." This slang, like "Chink" or "Chinaman," are derogatory words that should *NEVER* be used. This is the same with Japs, Portagee (For Portuguese) or kkadonam (Abrasive city man). Offensive! Racism language. The individuals of the given races take it very personally any may start a fight.

Case-Study 5

Internment Camps for the Japanese Americans:

As President Franklin D. Roosevelt called the unprovoked attack on Pearl Harbor a "date which will live in infamy." The Japanese Americans paid dearly for the attack. About 120,000 Japanese American citizens (Most of whom lived on the Pacific Cost) were forcibly relocated and incarcerated in concentration camps in the Western interior of the Country (Arizona, Arkansas, California, Colorado, New Mexico, Oregon, Utah, Washington and Wyoming). About 65% of the internees were United States citizens!

At the time, Executive Order 9066 was considered justified as a military necessity to protect against domestic espionage and sabotage. However, it was later documented that our government had in its possession proof that NOT ONE Japanese American, citizen or not, had engaged in espionage or any act of sabotage. Rather, the causes for this unprecedented horrific action in American history, according to the commission on Wartime Relocation and Internment of Civilians, were motivated largely by racial prejudice, wartime hysteria, and a failure of political leadership. Almost 50 years later, through the efforts of leaders and advocates of the Japanese- American community, Congress passed the *Civil Liberties Act of 1988*—popularly known as *the Japanese-American Redress Bill*. This law acknowledged that a grave injustice was done and mandated Congress to pay each victim of 80,000 internment victims $20,000 in reparations. Was this

JUSTICE when the internees took belongs that they could only carry on their backs, and suffered the harsh conditions at the camp? The mental and physical health impacts of the trauma of the internment experience continue to affect tens of thousands of Japanese Americans. Health studies have shown a two times greater incidence of heart disease and premature death among former internees, compared to non-interned Japanese Americans. There were many abuses; for instance, a routine contraband at the Santa Anita Assembly Center turned into a riot. Eager military personnel had become overzealous and abusive, which along the failure of several attempts to reach the camp's internal security chief, triggered mass unrest, crowd formation, and the harassing of the Japanese Americans. Military police with tanks and machine guns quickly ended the commotion. The overzealous military personnel were later replaced because of their cruel and racist actions. Congress sent letters of apologies to all 80,000 Japanese victims of the war.

The FBI searched the private homes of thousands of Japanese American residents on the West Coast, seizing items considered *'contraband.'* About 65% of Hawaii's population was of Japanese descent. In a panic, some politicians called for their mass incarceration. Because there were so many Japanese Americans, no internment camps were built on the Hawaiian Islands. However, some Japanese American residents were arrested and 1,500 people (1% of the Japanese population in Hawaii) were sent to internment camps on the mainland. Assembly Centers were located in remote areas, often reconfigured fairgrounds and racetracks featuring building not meant for human habitation—like horse stalls or cow sheds that were converted for that purpose. The Santa Anita Assembly Center had 18,000 incarcerated, 8,500 of whom lived in stables. Food shortages and substandard sanitation were prevalent at these facilities. The 10 internment camps were surrounded by barbed-wire fences with towers manned by Army soldiers with machine guns to prevent any internee from escaping.

The internees were treated harshly and cruelly. Some Japanese Americans died in the camps due to inadequate medical care and the emotional stresses they encountered. Several were killed by military guards for allegedly "resisting orders." The Japanese Americans—half of whom were children were incarcerated for up to four years without due process of law.

The last Japanese internment camp closed in March 1946. Present Gerald Ford officially repealed *Executive Order 9066* in 1976, and in 1988.

Case-Study 6

The All-Hawaii Battalion and Racism:

The Japanese American citizens were not able to enter WW-II because of their ancestry; they were classified as 4-C—unsuitable for service because of race or ancestry. On March 31, 1942, the nisei (2nd generation Japanese Americans) were expressly forbidden from being inducted into the armed forces. They petitioned Congress that they should be allowed to defend the United States because they were American citizens. There were reports of "Jap riots" at Tule Lake that were used by anti-Asian groups as proof of Japanese American disloyalty.[7] July 1, 1944, a bill was introduced to allow the Justice Department to denationalize Japanese Americans. However, on February 1, 1943, President Ted Roosevelt announced the formation of the 442nd Regimental Combat Team—an all Japanese-American unit. Also, on January 200, 1944, Secretary of War,

Henry Stimson, announced the reinstatement of the draft for all Nisei men (2nd generation Japanese Americans with citizenship). An estimated 33,000 Japanese Americans served in the U.S. military during WW II, of which 800 were killed. My uncle was killed fighting the war in Italy. He was trying to save the lost Texas Battalion surrounded by Germans deep in Italy. Today, Texas and Hawaii are sister states for friendship. The 100th/442nd Infantry Regiment became the most decorated unit in U.S. military history. The combat unit received over 4,000 Purple Hearts, 21 Medals of Honor, and an unprecedented seven Presidential Unit Citations.

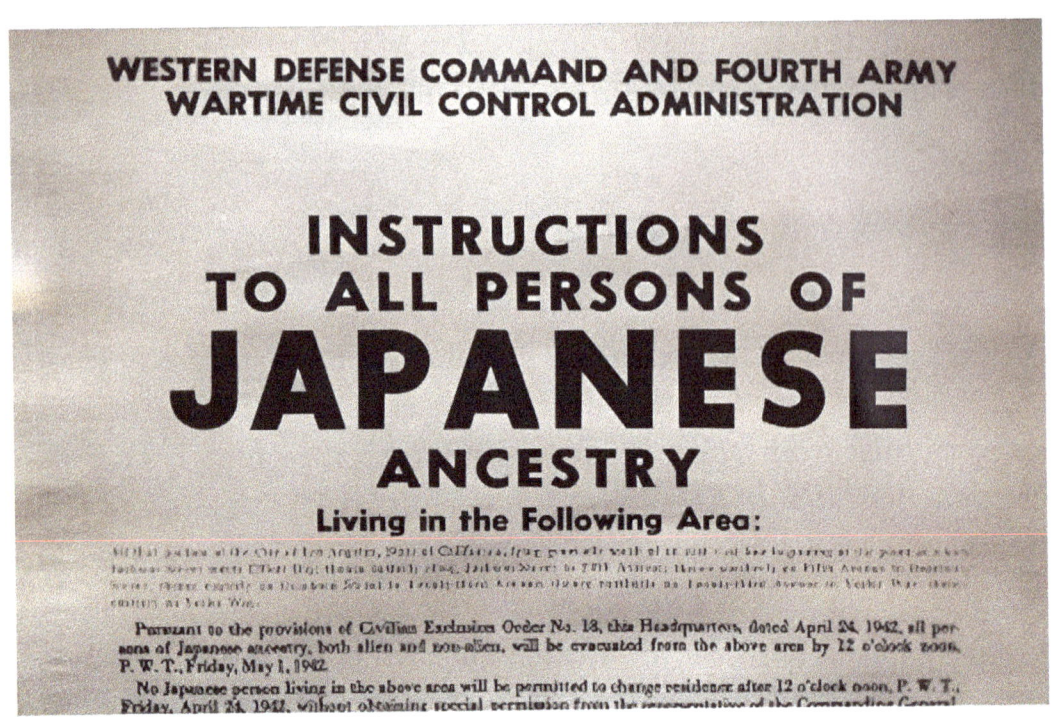

Photo 36. The United States government posted this type of notice to alert the Japanese-American citizens about their arrest as Internment prisoners.

Photo 37. Part of the 14,000 100th/442nd Regimental Combat Team (An all-Hawaii Japanese-American Unit) that fought in Europe.

The combat unit's motto was "Go for Broke". The motto was derived from a gambler's slang used in Hawaii to "go for broke," which meant that the player was risking it all in one effort to win big. The player would put everything on the line. It was an apt motto for the soldiers of the 442nd as they needed to put everything on the line to win big, the two wars—the war against the Germans in Europe and the war against racial prejudice in America. The Japanese Americans represented the largest ethnic group in the small island community of Hawaii.

Over time, Japanese Americans re-entered society and rebuilt their lives, families, and communities. In addition to returning to education, careers, starting families, and recuperating and healing from wartime injustices, they tried to demonstrate loyalty and their Americanness to the larger American public. Japanese Americans continued to fight remaining vestiges of institutionalized discrimination. In 1948, the U.S. Supreme Court decision in *Oyama vs. California* struck down provisions in California's Alien Land Law that prohibited Japanese immigrants from owning land[7]. Almost all Japanese Americans who had renounced their citizenship under duress, had their citizenship restored. Also, the Japanese American Citizens League formed an alliance with the African American Civil Rights groups like the National Association for the Advancement of Colored People (NAACP) in other 14th Amendment cases involving land ownership and housing[7].

It was September 1942, Bob Fuchigami and his siblings clambered out, trying to find their meager belongings. They sought out their parents and familiar faces as solders with bayonets on their rifles hustle them onto trucks and buses for a short ride into the barbed-wired perimeter of Granada Relocation Center. Guard towers loomed at the camp sites with solders with machine guns[5]. The Fuchigami family and thousands of Japanese-Americans in California had been rounded up by the U.S. government, detained in horse stables on rodeo grounds for months before being herded onto an Eastbound train for Colorado. There, in a desolate corner of the state near a town nicknamed 'End of the line,' the Federal government had hastily erected a smaller town known informally as Camp Amache, where the detainees would live out the remainder of WWII unless they spent time with the seven siblings who were all American citizens by birthright; it didn't matter. In the months following the attack on Pearl Harbor on December

7, 1941, the U.S. government, buoyed by a century of anti-Asian racism, forced more than 120,000 people of Japanese descent to leave their homes and businesses along the Pacific Coast. Tensions between White and Japanese Americans quickened as Japan entered WW-II in 1940. After the war, decades of lawsuits and complaints by Amache detainees and other internment camp Japanese Americans forced the Federal government to recognize their treatment was both illegal and immoral. Some Asian-American lawmakers warn that disparaging language framing China as a top economic competitor may spur a new wave of anti-Asian violence in America. Their concerns have grown in recent weeks as Congress has focused to a bill—known as the COMPETS Act, aimed at strengthening America's supply chain amid a shortage of goods. The bill often referred to as the *"China Competitiveness Bill,* or simply *The China Bill,* passed the House in early February 2022 by President Joe Biden[6]. The last time that the U.S. was in tensions and in conflict with an Asian superpower, the U.S. interned tens of thousands of Japanese Americans in internment camps so we don't have a great track record.

Case-Study 7

The Korean American-African American Riots:

The 1992 Los Angeles riots were horrific. Looting and arson began on April 29, 1992. The result of several days of rioting, more than 50 people were killed, more than 2,300 were injured, and thousands were arrested. About 1,100 buildings were damaged, and total property damage was about $1 billion, which made the riots one of the most-devastating civil disruptions in American history. This was sparked after a jury acquitted three Los Angeles police officers of use of excessive force for brutally beating Rodney King and failed to reach a verdict for a fourth officer. Included in that hate riots was the killing of Latasha Harling, a 15-yearold Black girl, by a Korean convenience store owner who said she stole a bottle of orange juice. The shop owner, Soon Ja Du, was sentenced to probation, community service and a $500 fine—a decision that was upheld a week before the uprising. Although many citizens of Los Angeles prided themselves on their city's ethnic diversity, many felt that the city's predominantly White police force practiced racial profiling and engaged in racist brutality against African Americans and Hispanic Americans. A videotape shot by a man who watched police officers brutally beat Rodney King to the ground failed, they clubbed him with their batons dozens of times. On April 29, 1992, protest and violence erupted almost immediately after the jury (composed of 10 Whites, a Hispanic American, and an Asian American) acquitted the police officers of charges that included assault with a deadly weapon and excessive use of force. Hundreds of protesters congregated outside the LA Police Department chanting, "No Justice, No Peace." There was also large-scale rioting that resulted in 34 deaths in 1965. The live television coverage captured an assault on a White-truck driver, who was pulled from the cab of his vehicle, beaten, and smashed with a cinder block. Reginald Denny, who was part of the news media, while trying to cover the news, made the incident more inflammatory with the kind of racial languages that were used. The news media must use restraint to minimize the sensationalism to obtain high viewer ratings.

This is one of the areas where we can greatly improve controlling racism (See chapter 11). The news media need to restrain themselves by not sensationalizing themselves to keep the rioting down to a minimum.

This is when "Black Lives Matter" movement started.

However, **"Asian-American lives Matters too"**.

Actually, **"All Lives Matter."**

"All colors under the rainbow matter."

Why can't we conduct our lives as if we are ALL **"Colorblind?"**

According to Eduardo Bonilla-Silva, most Whites in the United States rely on the ideology of color-blind racism to articulate their views, present their ideas, and interpret interactions with people of color[2]. For example, they believe Black Americans are culturally deficient, welfare dependent, and lazy. They regard affirmative action and reparation as tantamount to 'reverse discrimination.' Because Whites believe that they believe that discrimination is a thing of the past, minorities protestations about being racially profiled, experiencing discrimination in the housing and labor markets, and being discriminated against in restaurants, stores, and other setting are interpreted as 'excuses.' Following the color-blind script Whites support almost all the goals of the Civil Rights Movement in principle, but object in practice to almost all the policies that have been developed to make these goals a reality. Although they abhor what they regard as Blacks' self-segregation, they do not have any problem with their own racial segregation because they do not see it as a rational phenomenon. Does every single White person subscribe to the frames, racial stories, and style associate with colorblind racism? The answer is obviously not. Historically, racial progress in America has always transpired because of the joint efforts of racial minorities and White progressive. No one can forget the courageous efforts of Whites such as John Brown, Taddeur Stevens, Charles Summer, Lydia Maria Child and the many Whites who joined the Civil Rights Movement—no one should ever ignore White militants who struggled for racial equality and who risked their lives for this goal. Therefore, today, as with yesterday, a portion of the White population is not singing the true tune of color blindness.

Black Americans for the most part, do not subscribe wholeheartedly to the frames of color blindness. Furthermore, Blacks have oppositional views on many important issues. For example, they believe discrimination is a central factor shaping their life chances in this Country, firmly support affirmative action, and are very clear about Whites' advantageous position in this society. However, some of the frames and ideas of color blindness have had a significant indirect effect on Blacks. For example, the frame of abstract liberalism has shaped the way many Blacks explain school and residential segregation. The style of color-blind racism has had very limited impact on blacks. Where Whites hesitated the use double-talk to state their views on racial matters, Blacks state their views clearly and without much hesitation, even when the of discussion is interracial marriage. Only two of the four lines of color blindness have had some impact on some impact on Blacks. One of the latest in the news media are the eight killings of Korean Americans at three Atlanta-area spas by a 22-year-old boy, Robert Aaron Long on March 16, 2021:

    Soon Chung Park (Korean American died of gunshots to the head)

    Hyun Jung Grant (Korean American died of gunshots to the head)

    Suncha Kim (Korean American died of gunshots to the chest)

    Yong Ae Yue (Korean American died of gunshots to the head)

    Xiaojie Tan (Chinese American died of gunshots)

Delana Ashley Yaun (Chinese American died of gunshots)

Daoyou Feng (Chinese American died of gunshots)

Elcias Hernandez-Ortiz (Mexican American that survived the gun-shots in the face and spent a long time in the intensive- care ward)

Aaron Long used a 9mm semi-automatic pistol and was charged with 23 charges. He purchased the weapon for $460 at Big Woods Goods in Holly Springs, Georgia. After buying the gun, Aaron Long drove to a liquor store to purchase bourbon. He said, "what he did is against his Christian religion."

Case-Study 8

Mendez vs. Munemitsu:

This is a story of two immigrant families (Mexican American and Japanese American) their struggle against racism in WW-II era in California.[18] In the face of tremendous discrimination, the two families were sustained by the simple yet harrowing acts of kindness extended to them by friends and strangers as they navigated their difficult journeys toward justice. It is this kind of kindness that will encourage other people's hearts, open paths to solutions to discriminations, prejudices, and racisms, and create communities of support:[18]

Kindness is…going out of your way to help a friend.

Kindness is…being unifying and inclusive.

Kindness is…giving immigrants opportunities they would not normally have.

Kindness is…caring for the children of others as your own and letting the lines between family and friends' blur.

Kindness is…taking time to help others, no matter how young they are.

Kindness is…remembering those who helped you with gratitude.

Kindness is…collaboration and building trusted friendships.

Kindness is…neighbors helping neighbors; neighbors caring for their neighbor's belongings as if they were their own.

Kindness is…speaking out for the oppressed and standing against injustice, even despite the injustice that you yourself have experienced and endured.

Kindness is…keeping children safe and well, even children of another mother.

Kindness (omoiyari)[i]…is a Japanese word for sympathy and compassion shown and demonstrated for others.

Kindness is…words of compassion and encouragement when facing an unknown future.

Kindness is caring enough to help a friend find a solution to his problem.

Kindness is…using what you have to further what you believe.

Kindness is…sacrificing for the good of those you don't know, even the generations to come.

Kindness is…sacrificing your freedom to fight for the freedom of the whole community.

Kindness is…a community sharing difficult life experiences together.

Kindness is…friendship and car from strangers in faraway cities.

Kindness is…strangers becoming new friends for life.

Kindness…treating every human as human, understanding that everyone is "like us."

Kindness is…caring for those who have been discriminated against and looking for ways to welcome them into the community.

Kindness is…working together regardless who owns what.

Kindness is…collaborating together for a win-win solution.

Kindness is…sacrificing your time and effort for the sake of others.

Kindness is…loving friends of all colors.

Kindness is…seeing other people uniquely.

Kindness is…courage to stand for what is fair and just for all.

Kindness is…including others and being included.

Kindness is…sacrificing for the good of others.

Kindness is…standing together to fight against racism, no matter how difficult it gets.

Kindness is…standing up for those being oppressed because we are one human race.

Kindness is…looking beyond your own race in order to look out for others as well.

Kindness is…humbly admitting you made a mistake, even though years have passed.

Kindness is…persevering for what you believe without thought of any reward.

Kindness is…remembering what others have suffered with compassion and hospitality, even when you have suffered far worse. Kindness is…respecting our differences as one humanity.

Kindness is…an apology, though long—awaited and contested, given and accepted.

Kindness is…giving your own time to encourage and lift others up, Kindness is…understanding that racism can cause deep, painful, and long-standing wounds in the heart.

Kindness is…respecting people for who they are and not judging them by the color of their skin.

Kindness is…mutual respect and gratitude for each other.

Two professors from the American University—one White and the other Black. The white author grew up in an-White suburb of New York and currently lives in an all-White suburb of Washington, D.C. and knows almost nothing about the Black neighborhoods nearby. The Black author grew up in an all-Black neighborhood in Washington D.C. and now navigates between her predominantly White world of work and predominantly Black personal life. They both researched the topic—does their own experience epitomize the state of racial integration in America? They researched the topic for two years before publishing their book[28].

Through research, interviews, anecdotes, they probed the depths of integration's failure in America by exploring the ways we live, learn, work, and think. They addressed such crucial questions as to why Blacks and Whites see the world differently—why many Whites believe that discrimination is a thing of the past and why the Blacks seem so angry and why Whites avoid intimacy with the Blacks. The authors looked at our history, culture, media, and politics to understand how the myth of integration is still being perpetuated. They discussed integration success stories and asked whether they can translate it into the rest of society and the authors informed the readership what we can do to become a more racially honest nation.

Richard Thompson Ford[9] discussed how the law corrupts the struggle for equality. Civil rights are remarkably effective against overt prejudice perpetrated by identifiable bigots. But they have proven important against today's most severe social injustices, which involve covert and repressed prejudice or the innocent perpetuation of the past prejudice. Civil rights are indispensable tools—but sometimes they will do more harm than good.

One of the most insightful collections of information on racism is sequestered in a lively academic field known as critical race theory

(CRT)[7] which are *White supremacist* who believe that the only kind of racism that exists is "anti-White racism." Using **W**hat, **W**hen, **W**here, **W**hy and How White supremacy—which you'll be well ahead of the vast majority of the population, who have no idea what White supremacist racism really is, were it came from, or what could possibly be done about it. White supremacy is, most fundamentally a system of power designated to channel material resources to people socially defined as White people. Second, White supremacy is NOT just neo-Nazi and White nationalism. It is also the way our society has come to be structured, such that pollical, economic, and other forms of capital are predominately maintained by elite Whites. You probably grew up like everybody else that racism is mainly a thing of the past. As a friendly reminder, there is nothing new about the normalization of White supremacy in the United States. Second, White supremacy is the air we breathe—or don't breathe. It's embedded within our major institutions, our political economy, definitions of citizenship, our cultural codes and expectations, the very sources are distributed, and our physiological biases. White supremacist social arrangements and beliefs are woven into the fabric of our everyday lives. White supremacy is, in fact, so normal so systemic, pervasive, and taken for granted that it is almost never acknowledged, much less opposed, by members of the majority population. Thus, the idea that White supremacy ceased to exist in the distant past but then suddenly it has become more normalized in the last few years and is on face a lie—one sustained, primate by the KKK fallacy, as well as the Political Fallacy. I think that White people aren't aware that racism isn't just wearing White hoods and burning crosses. It's also fixing the system so that Black votes get counted. It's outlawing affirmative action at the state level even though it has proven successful.

Photo 38. Freedom is NOT Free; it certainly isn't when you have hated crimes in this Country.

Chapter 7
Multi-factorial Causes of Asian Racism

A. Effects of Past History:

Reviewing our past American history, it seems that we have always been a racist. Since the Puritanical days (16th and 17th centuries) we have had religious persecution and isolation. These spiritual groups even had racist attitudes with the American Indians. The history of racism in America is long—American Indians, American Eskimos, Black Americans, Chinese Americans, Japanese Americans, Korean Americans, Filipino Americans, Native Hawaiian/Pacific Islanders, Hispanic Americans.

B. Influence of Work Ethics:

Slavery was the *mode-of-operandi* with most cultures when immigrants arrived to America. This form of labor produced a lot of hate crimes the way the different immigrants were treated.

Anti-Asian crimes rise despite progress. Mass shooting took place in America amid a historic increase in violence against Asian Americans during the 2020-2022 coronavirus pandemic. Since then, the federal government has passed legislation to combat hate crimes, a Georgia prosecutor announced that she is seeking the death penalty for a 22year-old Atlanta gunman for killing four Asian Americans because of the state's new hate crimes law. President Joe Biden signed into law the *Covid-19 Hate Crimes Act* on May 2022, which expedites the Justice Department's review of hate crimes and offers grants to states to improve hate crimes reporting.

Even though state and federal laws impose additional penalties when a crime is motivated by racial bias, there is no evidence stiffer punishment deters Americans from committing these hate crimes according to Dr. Phyllis Gerstenfeld, a California State University professor who studies hate crimes. She said, "there is very little research on what strategies can effectively prevent prejudiced crimes because the motivating factors are so complex and it's difficult to predict who might commit these kinds of crimes. Most offenders are young, White men who have little criminal history, don't know their victims, and are not part of an organized hate group. She said education and improved messaging around tolerance is the best way to prevent violence. Unless we do something about the deeper causes, long term we're not going to have any solutions."

C. Education in the Public School System:

According to Alexander Alland, Jr.[1,11] *Project Head Start* was an attack on the governmental program, who's program goal was to help children from poor neighborhoods prepare for their entry into the regular school system through attendance at free government- supported preschools. The assumption behind Heart Start was that the children of the poor suffered a learning deficit in their early formative years due to an impoverished intellectual environment. For those who believed that IQ and, therefore, performance was hereditary, Head Start was seen as a waste of Federal monies. The program was criticized because IQ was largely hereditary and that the Black Americans were genetically inferior to White Americans. This theory was taken seriously among those holding political power in this Country. There is a flaw in the U.S. government census classification system. When it comes to African Americans, because the American folk system of racial classification system is based on the notion that "one drop of African blood puts one into that racial category," the traditional system of categorization was generally accepted, even though there have always been dissenters who refused to pick a single racial or ethnic label. Recent years we have seen more and more mixed marriages of various types—between racial groups, between religions, and between different ethnic groups. Tiger Wood, world champion golfer, who claims and does claim African, Southeast Asian, White, and American Indian ancestry. This identity shift was official in 2000 census, which for the first time, gave individuals an expanded laundry list of racial and ethnic groups which to identify. Additionally, people were able to check more than one category to proclaim their mixed heritage. The problem provides yet another example of how complicated the playing out of racial and ethnic identity is contemporary American society is. Until we have full equality of opportunity, until the barriers of de fact racial segregation are broken down, and until racial stereotyping of the kind described in this book ends, the problem will continue to remain part of the "American dilemma."

The new immigrant groups brought unfamiliar levels of diversity to the Asian-American sensibility, particularly where South Asians are concerned. Even

American-born second-generation Asian American debate whether to consider themselves Asian American.[30] The predominance of Chinese, Japanese, Koreans, and Vietnamese from East Asia often makes South Asians feel like outsiders in pan- Asian Americans settings—a situation made worse by East Asians who fail to recognize South Asia as part of Asia. Differences in physical features also come into play when, in archaic racial parlance, brown-complexioned South Asians are "Caucasoid" while yellow-toned East Asians are Mongoloid. Some South Asian Americans cite this racial distinction as a reason not to consider themselves Asian American. This was argued by the Punjabi immigrants. But who would have thought that taxicab drivers from Pakistan India, and Bangladesh could unite and lead a motley army of global immigrants? Many in New York view these taxicab drivers reckless and who spoke English with a strong accent, have funky smelling caps, are irritating, wear turbans and are rude. The cabdrivers have been cited for refusing to pick up Black passengers or go into Black neighborhoods—a charge that points to their own prejudices.

They have been accused of being reckless drivers. The public's attention was on the rising number of accidents involving Yellow Taxicabs. Between 1990-1996, according to the Taxi and Limousine Commission, accidents shot up 41%. For example, during 1977, 28 people were killed and 21,000 injured—many in illegal cabs. Mayor Rudolph Giuliani described the taxi drivers as "reckless, lawless, and as terrorists[26].

With all these different incidences, how can the public have a different view other than hate crimes. Unless these types of behaviors don't change, racism will continue to grow.

D. Influence of Being Different:

Why being different can agitate the person next to you? Is it better that the planet be aliens—all the *SAME* size, height, shape, color? What are the solutions to resolving discrimination, racism, prejudices?

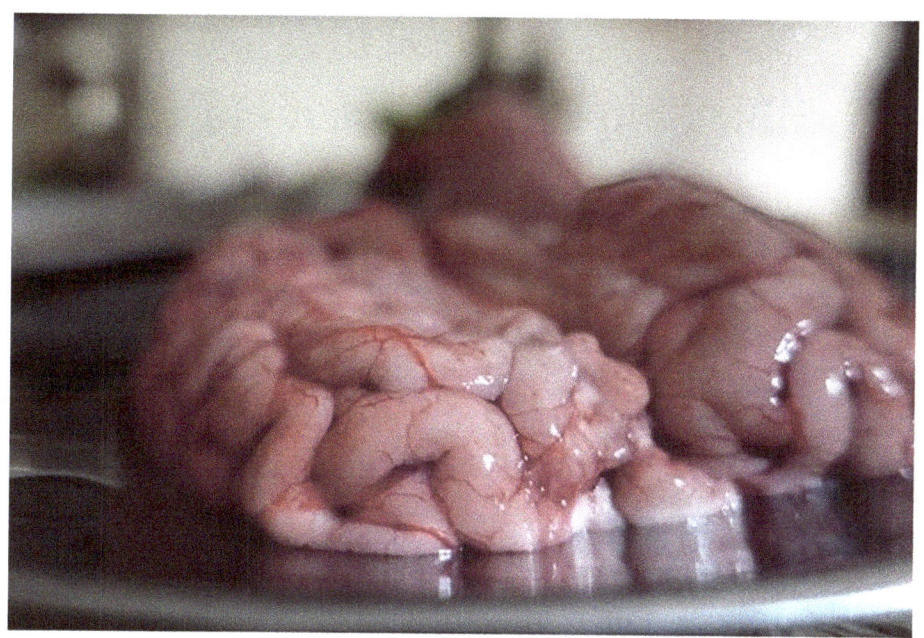

Photo 39. Eating different foods unlike the ordinary like pate, tripe, chitterlings, trotters, hog brains, you may be labelled being different and treated differently.

Why *differences* become problematic? Like your children eating vegetables and liking them, we need to train them early. Racism, hate crimes, and the like need to start as early as you can. Debra Van Ausdale and Joe R. Feagin[35] had the correct idea about educating children when they are young. I will have more to say on that important topic later.

Photo 40. This Asian-American girl looks different so she is being racially harassed.

Chapter 8
Possible Solutions to Asian Hate Crimes

Bullying is a form of hate crime. It is more common than thought. One in three children have been a victim at least one and adults are growing in numbers.

I am adding this topic in this book because it is a common phenomenon that children experience in daily life which is part of hate crimes. Bullying seeks to harm, intimidate, or coerce someone perceived as vulnerable; it is a blustering, browbeating person especially one who is habitually cruel, insulting, or threatening to others who are weaker, smaller, or in some way vulnerable tormented by the neighborhood or school bully, a pimp, a hired ruffian, or sweetheart. Bullying is a repeated physical, social, or psychological behavior that refers to the misuse of power by a person or group towards another individual or person. It is totally unacceptable in the United States or any country. However, acts of bullying are typical for the educational institutions, especially in the high schools. The most prevalent age of bullying occurs between 11-13 years (33%), followed by 8-10 years (2150, teens (20%), 6-7 years (5%), and 4-5 years (1%). 2020 research shows that girls and boys are both victims and aggressors of bullying.

Why is bullying so harmful?

What are the negative aspects and adverse consequences of bullying?

What mental and physical trauma can be caused by bullying?

What are the outcomes of bullying?

What is the school environment and bullying policies like?

What are the consequences of the bullying perpetrators and how are they treated?

What do they do to the bystanders who watched the bullying?

What kind of emotional and verbal aggressions are the perpetrators using?

What kind of conduct does your friends and peers tolerate?

Do you have a system in place that minimizes bullying? Does the social media contribute to the bulling?

Photo 41. A boy is taunting the girl who is being hurt (Is crying) because of the nasty bullying. According to the latest research, one out of three children is a victim of bullying, which is a hate crime. Why even do it? Do you do it?

Are Anti-Bullying programs effective? According to research, Antibullying programs reduce school-bullying perpetrations by about 20 percent. Do Federal anti-bullying laws? According to the Philippine government (RA 10627) the court decisions rules in favor of the plaintiffs in only 2% of the cases. So, this is only an initial step in the process.

Cyberbullying can affect anyone and may even cost their life. Cyber bullying victims have suffered drastically from some types of cyberbullying. Cyberbullying victims are more likely to have low self-esteem, depression, and more likely to consider suicide. Many young girls are forced to believe that society will not accept them unless their figure is identical to a model, changing their mentality to do unfortunate things towards their natural bodies. The social media has made it difficult for many young individuals to accept themselves for who they really are, and as a result it forces many of them to change themselves mentally and physically to be accepted to this changing society social media has been dreadfully created.

If you don't want to be bullied, don't do it to others. Go with the saying, "*Do unto Others as You Want Others to do onto You.*" These are hateful crimes; remember photo 6? You have choices—Positive or Negative. Making a person feeling crummy is not a good thing. Nothing good can come out of feeling bad. You want a photo showing smiles (Photo 42).

Photo 42. A young girl that is always smiling because of how she is treated with kindness by her peers.

Photo 43. Would you prefer to have teens free of hate crimes and racism?

Bullying can be done anywhere, anytime, even in the workplace.

Case-Study #1:

Ron works in a plumbing shop as an apprentice for six years and his boss, Eddie, called him gay and used offensive languages toward him. This is certainly an uncalled-for bullying and a hate crime filled with discrimination, prejudices, and racism, even.

Case-Study #2:

Eddie even encouraged the other employees to call him names, asked him inappropriate questions and make crude insinuations about his personal life, which is uncalled for under any circumstances.

Case-Study #3:

Eddie took his mobile phone and made him believe that he had posted inappropriate comments on a female friend's page. Do you believe that this is a case of bullying?

Case-Study #4:

Eddie had one of his employees put a live mouse down the back of Ron's shirt. This is hateful but, Is this a complaint for bullying?

Case-Study #5:

Ron was too afraid to complain to his manager. Was that correct? What else could Ron have done? What would you do if you were Ron? Ron took his case to the court and won under the Occupational Health and Safety Act 2004 and was awarded $12,500. The employees and Eddie were found guilty of risk in the workplace and workplace bullying. To drive the point home on workplace bullying I will enforce it with another series of Case-Studies at a local bakery where they were required to perform tasks including baking, sandwich preparations, general food preparation, cleaning and delivery of orders to different businesses:

Photo 44. **Fist Bumps:** *We need to show more physical friendship, especially between people with color.*

Case-Studies #A:

The owner, Mike, the boss, was in the baking business for over 25 years and he had one assistant, Sam wo was a timid and quiet individual.

Case-Study #B:

Over a two-year period, Sam was called 'pig," "porky," "dog'" and other derogatory names by Mike, who occasionally yelled and threw a temper tantrum for no reason at all. How did that make you feel?

Case-Study #C:

Sam was labelled as 'Useless' and 'a Waste of Space' by Mike. How did you sleep at night that evening?

Case-Study #D:

Sam was told many times, "To go away and die; and die quietly." How did you feel when your friend picked you up to drive you home after work?

Case-Study # E:

Sam went home a physical and mental wreck. Would feel the same way too? I know that I would feel horrible; however, I would say something! Sam filed with the court and was awarded $50,000 under the Occupational Health and Safety Act 2004. The Judge told Mike to knock off the workplace bullying!

Carrying this hate crime further, I will go into racism. The causes of racism is multi-factorial—but it is a *learned* behavior—which should be stopped when your child is young; stopping racism and hate crimes the earlier the better. I am going to list a limited number of celebrities because I am not promoting them; I am trying to make a point about race and racism—it can happen anywhere, it can happen to anyone: rich or poor, White or Black, Jewish or Muslim, famous or not-so-famous. Do you recognize any of these people?

*Photo 45. **Holding Hands:** If you wish to be friendlier to people of color, with their permission, or if you are having a personal relationship with the person—hold their hands—to demonstrate affection—to help show how much you care about people of color.*

Name Affected by Racism		
Race / Notible		
Profession / Worth		
Jennifer Lopez		
Puerto Rican-Grammy	American Latin Billboard	Emmy
Actress & Singer $400 M		
Dutchess Meghan		
Multiracial Actress		
Actress $10 M		
Michelle Obama		
Multiracial		Civil Rights Award
First Lady $70 M		
John Legend		
Multiracial Grammy	Academy	
Singer $45 M		
Thandie Newton		
Multiracial Emmy		
Actress $14 M		

> Lucy Lui
>
> Chinese-American Emmy
>
> Actress $16 M

A. *Collecting Accurate Data by Having the Public Participate in Symposia to Voice their Opinions on What Causes Hate Crimes:*

We need more accurate data from the public on why we have so much hate crimes. Setting up committees of experts is simply not enough. Having committees of experts on racism are necessary, but to help get to the root cause of racism, we need the victims' thought processes. Hate crimes are a multifactorial cause and we need all the data we can possibly gather. "No stone should be left unturned."

B. *Redefine Racism Education:*

The education system should be the forefront of the battle to combat racial inequality. Through careful consideration of the complex and pervasive nature of racism, we need the freedom to speak openly about the root causes and solutions by having state and federal government officials, parents, experts on hate crimes, children, and victims attend these meetings. School educational policies must be changed to be broader to allow new avenues to explore and discuss the new territories that need to be explored.

We need more state and federal funding to do more research on causes and solutions that the schools (Grade school through college) can use to educate our children on racism.

One method of gathering data and teaching the concepts of anti- hate crimes is gather in small groups to have dynamic discussions about these hate crimes on why they happen, how we prevent its occurrences, and how to be a positive role model.

Using tools such as movies and videos on hate crimes can be fruitful at all grade levels. Having school homework on racism and having the students read their research in the classroom is another route to use to motivate children and young adults about practicing anti-racism.

C. *Outcomes of Inter-rational Marriages:*

Inter-racial marriages are becoming more common today. You would think that this would propel the progress of anti-racism. You see White grandparents with biracial grandchildren everywhere now, something that was rare and not that many years ago. According to the United States Census Bureau, the number of interracial married couples increased from 310,000 in 1970 to more than 2 million in 2008. According to Pew Research Center, the share of married Blacks with a spouse of a different race has tripled from 5% in 1980 to 18% in 2018. The American Indians have the highest Interracial marriage rate among all groups. The second most common intermarriage pairing is among Whites and Asians. The numbers are still growing.

Are we getting less hate crimes? You are wrong! There are numerous hate crimes that are thrown onto the couples from flattening tires when the couples are eating at a restaurant to not talking to their biracial neighbor.

Interracial relationships still stir racist passions. For instance, in 1992, A volunteer coordinator of Patrick J. Buchanan's Republican presidential campaign in New Jersey was removed after he compared mixed marriages to the cross-breeding of animals. This is likely to be even more true as the nation's Hispanic American and Asian American populations continue to grow. Many of the new immigrants came from countries with mixed-race traditions. Some analysts say that makes them more open to interracial marriage, particularly to Whites. In much of Latin America, marrying a person of lighter skin color is considered a move up the social ladder. Today, almost one-third of the U.S.-born Hispanics ages 25-34 are married to non-Hispanic Whites. In addition, 36% of young Asian Pacific American men born in America marry White women and 45% of U.S.-

born Asian Pacific American women took White husbands. The vast majority of Native Americans also married Whites. The bumpy road with the mixed-marriage couples continued endlessly. According to the 1990 census, almost one in three of the children whose fathers were White and mothers as Black identified themselves as White. That was a 50% increase over the 1980 census. Similarly, the children of White fathers and Japanese or Chinese mothers were listed as White according to the 1990 census.

We need to work together to form a unified and peaceful community to help reduce the number of hate crimes.

D. *Make an Effort to Work on Community Projects of Different Ethnic Backgrounds:*

Just like **The Humana Projects**, which is a nonprofit organization that work in 45 countries across five continents. They have implemented more than 1,453 developmental projects. The organization believe in the power of the people working together to bring about lasting change, using simple, strong and low-cost developmental concepts that can be scaled up. The Foundation invested $5.4 million in eight communities across the Southeastern United States to address social determinants of health on a local level—helping more people achieve health equity as part of its ongoing *Strategic Community Investment Program. The Humana Foundation 2020 programs* include the following:

New Orleans, LA: Kingsley House received $341,000 for its Career Pathways program, which creates greater financial asset security and post-secondary attainment and sustaining employment. The Kingsley House will collaborate with DePaul Community Health Centers and Crescent City Family Services to help families access community resources.

Growing Local Food Collaborative received $600,000 to address financial asset security, post-secondary attainment and sustaining employment, and food security in New Orleans. Partners in this initiative include Liberty's Kitchen, New

Orleans Food Policy Action Council, Recirculating Farms Coalition, Strout NOLA, and Top Box Foods Louisiana.

Baton Rouge, LA: Healthy BR received $675,000 to continue improving food security and social connectedness via the Geaux Get Healthy project, and with the help of Glue Cross Blue Shield of Louisiana Foundation. This project addresses food deserts by saturating these areas with numerous access points for purchasing fresh food at an affordable price. HOPE Ministries received $200,000 for its workforce development program, The Way to Work.

Broward County, FL: The Boward Health Centers received $400,000 to screen their patients for food security and diet-related disease. Engaging Patients Impacting Care (EPIC) will also help people apply for Supplemental Nutritional Assistance Program (SNAP) benefits and help people access healthy foods via a produce prescription program.

Jacksonville, FL: The University of Florida received continued funding of $600,000 for Health-Smart, a holistic health program that promotes social connection and food security, and mental and physical health among Black seniors in underserved Jacksonville communities. Empowering these communities to bring about policy changes for transportation justice is also a program priority. Major program partners include twenty Black churches that are Health-Smart sites, University of Florida-Health—Jacksonville and its community Health Centers at Soutel and Durkeeville, Foodery Farms, Feeding North East Florida, the Jacksonville Urban League, and the local American Heart Association.

Knoxville, TN: Interfaith Health Clinic received $750,000 to continue its Truck-2 Table program, addressing social determinants of health and improving health and quality of life of uninsured and underserved people by providing affordable access to healthy foods, free-nutrition education and access to social connectedness resources.

Louisville, KY: The Family Scholar House received $300,000 for its HEROES program, which helps families and senior citizens to address social isolation, food insecurity, and lack of post-secondary educational attainment. Metro United Way also received $300,000 to continue AcceLOUrate Savings financial literacy program, improving financial independence and providing families and residents experiencing economic distress with financial literacy coaching and other social services.

San Antonio, TX: Older Adults Technology Services (OATS) received $150,000 to continue its Senior Planet San Antonio program, addressing social connectedness by engaging seniors through free access to internet-connected technology and training courses. The San Antonio Food Bank received $600,000 to continue its Healthy Options for the Elderly (HOPE) program, assisting seniors who screen positive for food security and social connectedness concerns with comprehensive services that stabilize their household and address prevalent health issues.

Tampa, FL: Feeding Tampa Bay program received $530,000 to continue work to transform affordable access to healthy foods in partnership with local clinics and other social service providers via the Feed Tampa Bay Food & Pharmacy programs. Community Health Centers of Pineball (CHIP) will continue as a key partner in this work with their onsite program, which increases access to healthy foods for the neighborhood surrounding the clinics.

Each organization that receives Humana Foundation Strategic Community Investment has the opportunity to receive continued funding for up to three years based on the specific results achieved in their programs, as well as other resources, such as skilled volunteers and opportunities to share organization learnings.

The Humana Foundation was established in 1981 as the philanthropic arm of Humana Inc. It is one of the nation's leading health and wellbeing companies that is located in Louisville, Kentucky. The foundation seeks to co-create communities where leadership, culture, and systems work to improve and sustain positive health outcomes. Humana and The Humana Foundation are dedicated to Corporate Social Responsibility. Their goal is to ensure that every business decision they make reflects their commitment to improving the health and well- being of their members, their employees, the communities that they serve, and the planet.

I mention the efforts of the Humana Foundation because I believe that they serve as a role model in a dynamic way to identify and solve problems on race and racism. We need similar sponsorships to help resolve hate crimes and racism. If we rely on local, state and federal governments for help we will be stuck in the dilemma we are in presently. We can't afford to wait because we are in a crisis. We need to act NOW! We need to have organizations and individuals to step up to the plate and help resolve Racism of all colors. How do we start?

E. *Seek the support of anti-prejudice and anti-racist organizations:*

We can start by soliciting *philanthropic* individuals who have a genuine interest in helping this planet conquer hate crimes because of skin color or differences in cultures. We can start with asking for financial help from the following individuals to create anti-hate programs:

Elon Musk of Tesla Motors ($1 trillion)

Jeff Bezos of Amazon ($177 billion)

Bernard Arnault of LVMH ($158 billion)

Bill Gates of Microsoft ($124 billion)

Larry Page of Google ($111 billion)

Sergey Brin of Google ($107 billion)

Larry Ellison of Oracle ($106 billion)

Mark Zuckerberg of Facebook ($97 billion)

Warren Buffet Berkshire Hathaway ($96 billion)

Steve Ballmer of Microsoft ($91.4 billion)

Mukesh Ambani of Diversified investment ($90.7 billion)

Gautam Adani of Infrastructure ($90 billion)

Michael Bloomberg of Bloomberg LP ($82 billion)

Carlos Slim Helu of Telecom ($81.2 billion)

Francoise Bettencourt Meyers of L'Oreal's Founder ($78 billion)

Ma Huateng of Tencent Internet ($65.8 billion)

Alice Walton of Walmart ($65.3 billion)

Jim Walton of Walmart ($61 billion)

Julia Koch of Koch Industries ($60.6 billion)

Rob Walton of Walmart ($60 billion)

Jack Ma of Alibaba (56.3 billion)

Mackenzie Scott of Amazon ($53 billion)

Daniel Gilbert of Quicken Loans (($52 billion)

Phil Knight of Nike ($50 billion)

Zhang Yiming of BiteDance and TikTok ($50 billion)

Julia Koch of Koch Industries ($46 billion)

Charles Koch of Koch Industries ($46 billion)

Masayoshi Son of Japanese multinational SoftBank (44.4 billion)

Takemitsu Takizaki of Keyence; bar-code readers (32 billion)

Jacqueline Mars of candy and pet foods ($31.7 billion

Cina Rinehart of Mining ($30.2 billion)

Shiv Nadar of Software Services ($28.7 billion)

Miriam Adelson of Casinos ($27.5 billion)

Susanne Klatten of BMW and Pharmaceuticals ($24.3 billion)

Cyrus Poonawalla of Vaccines ($24.3 billion)

Iris Fontbona of Mining ($22.8 billion)

Abigail Johnson of Money Management ($21.2 billion)

Radlhakishan Damani of Retail and Investments ($20 billion)

Lakshmi Mittal of steel ($17.9 billion)

Savitri Jindal of steel ($17.7 billion)

Kumar Birla of commodities ($16.5 billion)

Dilip Shanghvi of pharmaceuticals ($15.6 billion)

Uday Kotak of Banking ($14.3 billion)

Melinda French Gates of Microsoft ($12 billion)

Peter Briger of Fortress Investment group (10.7 billion)

Nassef Sawiris of Orascom Construction Industries (8.7 billion)

Akira Mori of Real estate developer (5.5 billion)

Wes Eden of Fortress Investment Group, Milwaukee Bucks Co-owner (4.62 billion)

Michael Jordan of Chicago Bulls (2.2 billion)

Vadim Novinsky of Akhmetov's Metinvest (2.2 billion)

Paul McCartney of the Beatles (1.2 billion)

F. *Be a Role Model: Add stricter laws with punishments that will discourage racism:*

As of 1999, 41 states and the District of Columbia have hate-crime statues that provide enhanced penalties for crimes in which victims are selected because of a perpetrator's bias against a victim's perceived race, religion, or ethnicity. Hate crime definitions often encompass not only violence against individuals or groups, but also crimes against property –such as arson or vandalism, particularly those directed against community centers or houses of worship.

Every effort should be made to exemplify youths who conduct proper behaviors in preventing hate crimes. The police, teachers, churches, and news media should play a more active role in selecting these youths and making public announcements to the news media. We need more role models to not only reward good behaviors, but to give examples of youths demonstrating voluntary activities on how to prevent crimes against skins of different color. Children learn by different methods: visual, auditory, exploratory, self-discovery, feeling. We need to provide many different tools of learning such as videos, illustrated books, and audio tapes. Have creative homework for the children to take home so the parents can get involved.

G. Be a Proactive Parent:

Whenever a racial incident happens with your child, report it immediately so the school administrators and the police can investigate the crime and prosecute the perpetrator(s), and have corrective policies created to protect others. Most children participate in sports at school and at extracurricular activities at churches and through other outlets. There are a growing number of minorities that participate in many competitive sports.

While it is important that your child learns the mechanics and techniques of the sport, do not neglect the fundamentals of good sportsmanship.[19] Why is practicing the fundamentals of good sportsmanship so important? Because it is a reflection of your child's true character—especially under bad or unsuccessful circumstances. The child's fellow teammates will accept your child more readily and respect him/her despite the color of their skin, rather than constantly avoiding them—and even having prejudices because of his/her bad sportsmanship conduct. As one famous athlete, Lori Myers, once said, "true sportsmanship is excellence in motion." As a parent, if you observe bad sportsmanship being done by the athlete, coach, referee, other students, and even by parents, call time out and bring it to the attention of someone who can officially stop such conduct— especially if done by an individual of color. If they think that they can get away with it, it is a journey to racism.

Like learning to eat something that your child dislike eating (Brussel sprouts, turnips, rutabagas), start them early. Follow the four elements for a faster learning curve—**W**hy, **W**hen, **W**here, and **H**ow[21]; be sure to always reward them whenever they do a good anti- racism deed. Never reprimand or use negative comments to your child when they say something racist to protect their self-esteem, according to Maslow's Hierarchy of Needs.[21]

Ages 0 to 5 years:

Your task is to provide positive groundwork by being an excellent role model. You can address *hate* by substituting *compassion* and *tolerance*. Teach them the innocent indifference to what sets people apart. Kids are born colorblind; look in the school yards and in the playgrounds, they play with their school mates of all different colors;[16] Dr. David Schonfeld, Professor of Pediatrics at the University of Southern California and Children's Hospital at Los Angeles said, "they don't discriminate." You can request that their teacher build multiculturalism into their curriculum. Speak your own native tongue in your home because a 2014 study by the University of Chicago revealed that children who hear multiple languages in daily life are more accepting of people whose languages differs from their own— is a stepping-stone toward a broader spirit of acceptance. Kids experiences a whole range of emotions— anxiety, panic, worries, anger, frustration, kindness, misapprehensions, fears, etc. Work with one or two of these emotions and work together by resolving the anti-racism. For a faster learning curve, include these four key pillars in your discussions—**W**hy, **W**hen, **W**here, and **H**ow[21] Remember to always reward your kids with something worthwhile when they execute a deed that is positive and correct[21]—especially when it comes to anti-racism. I always use this philosophy when coaching kids skiing.

Ages 6 to 11 Years:

Children at this age group are attuned to what is fair and what is not fair; this should be a strong basis for discussing *injustices*—like discrimination, prejudices, and racism.[16] Kids at this age can more precisely articulate their feelings. Ask them, how do they really feel about different multicultural public events. For example, take your child to an Asian American home where they are required to take their shoes or slippers off to enter their house. Have your child try different ethnic foods and do ask them what they think and feel. Trying and understanding different cultures is critical to expanding your kids' view of things in life. The more the better; you may even uncover that your child has misunderstood part of what has occurred. Be honest and opened when deliberating any racial topic. If you don't know the answer, do look it up. Do NOT use anything negative to protect his/her self-esteem. You could say, "I understand why you'd think that way, but what about his/her perspective?" Have you taken your kid to a Chinese New Year (*Kung See Fat Choy*) dragon dance or Japanese Obon ceremonial dance festival to drive away the evil spirits? Have you experienced any Korean festival to observe the country's history and heritage—Jeju Fire Festival, Jinju Lantern Festival, Hwacheon Sancheoneo Ice Festival, Gunhangje Cherry Blossom Festival, Boryeong Mud Festival, Busan International Film Festival?

Ages 11-18 years:

Children today have mobile phones at this age and they have access to limitless information. As a parent, you could be of great benefit to them by checking their understanding and interpretations of the racial concepts that they see and hear.[16] Take for instance, *racial bullying;* what would you tell your child if one of them said, "students at school are teasing the Hispanic kids?" First of all is it truthful? Perhaps, one can call the parents and talk to the Hispanic victims and together work on non-violent solutions. You can also play a game called **KINDNESS**—to help decrease the threat of hate-crime behaviors. What are the many ways that you can show and deliver kindness to the bullies? This is not backing down and not supporting what is correct. As a parent you need to be a role model and show your kids ways you can be effective when working against racism.

Do Random Acts of Kindness—especially if the individuals are of different color, different culture, speak a different language, or simply being *different!* The list can be endless, but here are some thoughts:

Give lots of hugs.

Provide positive comments (i.e., "You look terrific.").

Purchase a cup of java when you buy one for yourself.

Share your winter coat when it is extra cold.

Give a toy to a friend visiting you. Bake a pie for your neighbor.

Visit your student at the hospital.

Treat your cousin's friend to a movie.

Pick up a person every Sunday for church.

Wash the clothes of a visitor when he/she accidently spills food on their white shirt.

Create time to listen to a person's dilemma.

Help a person fix his/her vacuum cleaner.

Give assistance with your child's friend's homework.

Provide $50 when your son and friend go to the amusement park.

Help sell raffle tickets to the public for a rape-crisis center.

Donate money to a mental-health center.

Show *respect* to everyone; we all deserve it.

Give your friend a ride to the pharmacy at midnight.

Puppy sit for a friend in a neighborhood that is considered predominantly a Black community.

Volunteer for an Asian-American organization.

Help your Hispanic friend change her tire in the rain.

Teach a class on discrimination, prejudices, and racism for the summer at summer camps.

David Gillborn[11] obtained a grant from British Petroleum (BP) to do research on anti-racism in England. His focus was on West Indians or what's considered Asians in the British Isles, which went through major reforms under Margaret Thatcher, especially through the Education Reform Act (ERA) during 1988 and John Major through the *Education Act of 1993*. This marked the beginning of a distinctive new phase in the British education policy. It took the Thatcher government the best part of a decade to turn their attention fully to education. *The 1988 Act* established the legal framework for the imposition of a centrally defined 'National Curriculum; the introduction of a national system of testing a certain 'key age' (Years seven, 11, 14, and 16). It was accepted that there were some White people (A small minority) that harbored irrational prejudices against ethnic minorities, but this was seen as a personal failing, a result of ignorance, that should be handled carefully so as not to provoke any backlash. This view effectively defined the existence the possibility that impersonal rules and traditions, the very structures of society, might act in 'racist' ways.

This minimalist perspective on racism can be observed in the Report of the Elton Committee of Enquiry, Discipline in Schools. The report acknowledged evidence of 'racist attitudes among pupils' and even 'a few teachers.' One of the main innovations in the *1993 Act* was the establishment of a Funding Agency for Schools (FAS). This body administers the payment of funds to Grant Maintained schools and, under certain circumstances, shared or took over local authority's duties with regard to the school places. The other major advances were in quantitative research, which charted general patterns of success/failure, but began to unglue **W***hy* the hate patterns came about.

According to Gillborn,[11] anti-racism in symbolic gestures is meaningless. If the school does not involve the total community, teachers, ancillary staff, students and parents, both Black and White, in the efforts to tackle racism in school, the whole exercise will end in failure. Racism is a way of life in contemporary England. Education alone cannot remove racism from society; but as one of the major agencies through which we learn our place and sometimes stake a claim to a different one —those of us working in the educational system have both an opportunity and responsibility to struggle where we are. In addition, his research indicates that Asian racism can occur anywhere—even in another country like England. Is there anywhere on this planet where racism, prejudices, or discrimination does *NOT* exist?

According to Van Ausdale & Feagin[35] children can learn race and racism as early as preschool. The learning curve can be influenced by their environment: (1) the kids they play with, (2) the attitude of the teachers, (3) the behaviors of their parents, and (4) other adults. The interactions of these four components are primal to the social relationships. Society does not consist of individuals, but expresses the sum of the relationships in which individuals find themselves, and this is true for children as well as adults. The larger social and cultural fields in which children find themselves are not of their own making; they are, initially put into these fields without their input. They must then cope with the involuntary social fields created by their elders, and learn their meanings and negotiations. As they proceed into preschool settings, young children learn to move from the social field of interaction that is the family to the new social field of the school, a field that most will operate in for the next 15 to 20 years of their lives. Both social fields have many lines of forces with varying attraction and repulsions, lines and styles of communication and learning settings. Note that these two fields are both immersed in the larger field of the broader society. Yet very young children learn to cope effectively and, over time, successfully with all these social fields. Indeed, their attitude, personality, environment, exposure to race and racism and life-coping styles are developed and formed in these social fields.

Adults use racial and ethnic understandings to define themselves. From the typical White adult's perspective, children are generally not expected to employ ideas about racial group or ethnicity as part of serious self-definitions until they are well along toward adolescence. On the other hand, Van Ausdale & Feagin[35] strongly believe that throughout a life span the ideas, feelings, and language of racial group and ethnicity hold central importance in a person's self- definition and self-concept. For children, racial group and ethnicity become pertinent to self-conception and self-definition as they begin to interact with people inside and outside of their families. Hence, young children learn about race and racism almost immediately unless they live in isolation up in the Himalayan Mountains.

What are children's views on color? The complexity of what color means to children's evaluation of self, and what the self might look like will vary greatly from person to person.[16] The color of the hair, the color of the eyes, the color of the skin color, the shape of the eyes, are all determining factors. While it has never been researched or studied, my limited interviews with children suggest that if an individual have the combination of having an hour-glass figure plus having the looks of Miss Universe, or a voice of a nightingale, they are less confronted with race and racism.

What can preschool and elementary school teachers do? First, each teacher should make sure that she/he deals with personally racist inclinations and actions, no matter how *subtle*.[33] Second, take instances of racist talk or discriminatory behavior on the part of your children very seriously. Young children's ideas or race and ethnicity are often much more sophisticated and organized than most adults assume. Cultivate good and healthy attitudes that recognizes and acknowledges respect for peoples' differences.

What can parents do to break down the racial and ethnic barriers in this society? Parents need to create the truly fair and just society that we often proclaim. Educate yourself about the realities of racial discrimination against various racial and cultural groups and about the many aspects of individual and institutional racism. As a parent, you can actively form friendships with adults who belong to other ethnic and racial groups. Your goal is not to join the group to patronize the group, but to approach your efforts to make new friends with the intention of discovering good company in new places.

Recognize and encourage children's curiosity and their abilities to explore the social world with a sense of fairness. Accept the fact that most youngsters have much more social insight and understanding than adults would like to admit. In the grooming process, educate the kids to make this country a better place to live—once free of discrimination and inequality, prejudices, and racism.

What is totally ironic is when lighter skin people spend billions of dollars getting their skin color 50-shades of Brown, by going to self-tanning spas or using tanning lotions. **Why?** *Yet, these darkened individuals still practice racism!* Go figure!

Showing respect to everyone regardless of skin color or culture it is a forgotten art. We need to all strive to do better to close the gap on antiracism; it is one way we can show respect to a person and that we are kind and considerate:

Practice active listening to show you respect them: Watch and be quiet when someone else is talking and spend the time thinking about what they're actually saying. Nod your head if you agree and ask follow-up questions if you don't agree. Too often, we often make the error by jumping in to state our opinions first—especially if our ego is overblown. You might not agree, but you can respect it: When talking with someone and you disagree on something, don't take it personally. Try to remember that everyone has a different background and own reasons for thinking whatever they think. A good way to empathize with someone you don't agree with is to say, "Okay, I never thought it that way, let me try to understand by discussing with you further."

Try to validate their opinions: let them know that their opinions matter. When you validate people and their achievements, you are showing them that you respect their opinions and hard work.

Don't insult any opinions or ideas if you disagree with them: Instead, acknowledge your common ground before sharing your views. Be specific with your critique, and avoid simple or insulting language like, "You're wrong!" or "That's dumb!" Whenever making negative comments to a person, you need to always protect their self-esteem. Apologize when you're in the wrong: Saying, "I'm sorry" goes a long way; but say it with genuine feeling and that you really mean it. You want to display a great deal of maturity and not show disrespect. Do let people around you know that you will not tolerate disrespect or someone displaying rudeness: you can say something like, "I saw and heard you say what you said to Amy earlier and it seemed kind of rude. I just wanted to let you know that your comment came off as really disrespectful, even though you might not have meant it that way."

Compliment the achievements of others: draw attention the achievements and highlights of others around you to celebrate the good deeds that they have done; this reward will promote others to do the same.

Do what you say you'll do: Stick to your word to show other people respect: If you commit to an event or make plans with someone, come through on your end of the deal. Being reliable shows respect for people's time, and shows that you're making a special effort to be there for them. Respect other people's efforts by being on time, being prepared, and being enthusiastic on what you promised.

Offer your assistance to others: Don't isolate you help to just a few select individuals. For example, if it seems like one of your friends is feeling down or going through a rough time, give them the encouragement that they might need; don't neglect his wife if she needs help too.

Give yourself the same consideration you would give to others: Treat yourself a treat; your physical rest and mental health rest are important to be able to be useful to others. Set aside a few minutes every day to practice healthy selfcare.

Avoid self-destructive behaviors:

They can tear you mind and body down. Drinking beyond your ability to control yourself is a no, no.

Pay particular attention to older individuals: They especially need a lot of help because of the decline of their Cognitive, Affective (Emotional), and Physical (CAP) developments*21*. The average elderly person consumes seven medications daily, which can affect their daily living. For example, if he/she is a diabetic, they usually have hypertension (High-blood pressure) in addition. The first line medication is usually a diuretic like hydrochlorothiazide, which requires frequent urination (To lower the plasma volume and thus, lower blood pressure). Also, they move much slower and require assistance because of the loss of balance.*22* Be patient with them and show tolerance because of their age. These elderly people need your help and patience. Showing kindness to them is the correct way to make America the loving place to live.

Layla Saad[29] believes awareness leads to action, and action leads to change and that it can be accomplished in 28 days—by following a daily step-by-step detailed workbook. She is an East African, Arab, British, Black, Muslim woman who live and work in ways that leave a legacy of healing and liberation for those who will come after she is gone. Her focus in her book has been on the Black, Indigenous, and People of Color (BIPOC). She contends that White supremacy is a racist ideology that is based upon the belief that White people are superior in many ways to people of other races and therefore, white people should be dominant over other races. White supremacy is not just an attitude or a way of thinking. It also extends to how systems and institutions are structured to uphold this White dominance. Her research is not just about changing how thinks look but how things actually are—from the inside out, one person, one family, one business, and one community at a time. So, what can you personally do to stop racism?

Being colorblind— is a myth with many of the White supremacist in America who are racist. Most Whites assert they don't see any color, just people; although the ugly face of discrimination is still here.

How do racist stereotypes show up? Here are some examples of racist stereotype words sometimes associated with different groups:

Poor

Less educated

Less intelligent

Exotic

Spicy

Spiritual

Sexist

Oppressed

Terrorist

Drug dealers

Domineering

Effeminate

Aggressive

Demure

Alcoholics

Marijuana

Overachieving

Helpless

Hopeless

Opportunistic

Owning White privilege and being conditioned by the system of White supremacy mean that you have some subconscious values that are White supremacist in nature. For example, being conditioned within White supremacy means that of the values that you likely have is about White superiority—the idea that as a person with White privilege, you are more worthy and deserve to take up more space and resources that BIPOC. At the same time, you may have chosen value that says that you believe that all people are equal and deserve to be treated equally. This conflict of values make you question whether it means *you to be a good White person*.

H. *Support Anti-Prejudice and Anti-Racist Organizations:*

Racial equality will never be achieved by a single person or group. It takes a variety of activities, organizations, and approaches to create the necessary changes. As of today, there are over 350 anti-racist organizations; I will list a few:

The National Association for the Advancement of Colored People (NAACP) was founded in 1909 in response to the ongoing violence against Black people around the Country. It is the largest civil rights organization with over 2 million activists involved in its 2,200 units throughout America. Its mission is to secure the political, educational, social, and economic rights of Black people and to eliminate race-based discrimination and racism.

The Las Americas Immigrant Advocacy Center is a nonprofit organization that works to serve the legal needs of low-income immigrants who are not able to afford legal assistance. This organization helped people in Texas and New Mexico; it has served over 30,000 low-income immigrants in the El Paso area alone.

The American Civil Liberties Union (ACLU) seeks to ensure constitutional freedoms for every gender, race, and sexual orientation. Common issues include free speech, human rights, racial injustice, and criminal justice. The ACLU is composed of hundreds of attorneys and thousands of volunteers who are committed to protecting civil liberties in the country by continuing to lobby for systemic change across the Country.

Kids in Need of Defense (KIND) protects immigrant children by providing legal and social services to children who have crossed the U.S. border by themselves. It strives to make sure that no child appears in court alone. The members of KIND work to advance the laws around children's rights in America and offer several resources on how a adult can get involved. They also advocate for legal changes that protect vulnerable children who enter the U.S. themselves or those who are detained and separated from their families.

Advancement Project is a civil rights organization whose mission is to fulfill America's promise of caring, inclusive, and just democracy. The organization uses innovative tools to strengthen social movements and achieve high-impact policy changes. Advancement Project is involved in a variety of different campaigns and provides multiple opportunities for volunteers to get involved in various projects.

Color of Change is an online racial justice organization whose goal is to mobilize its members to knock down walls that hold back Black people. This organization was founded after Hurricane Katrina when they discovered that there were not enough resources dedicated to protecting and assisting Black people, who experienced devastating loses. Since then, they have started addressing police brutality against the Black community by leading campaigns to deter elected officials from supporting, investing in, and protecting an unaccountable police force. They are actively working on developing people-powered movements that will make a difference.

Live Free USA wants to reduce gun violence and county jail incarcerations. With over 118 million people attending weekly faith-based services in over 350,000 congregations across America, its aim is to create social justice by reaching churches. The goal is to end gun violence, mass incarceration and criminalization of Black and Brown people. According to Jim Willis[35] racism is a sin; preach it—teach it. *The National Coalition of Black Civic participation* seeks to encourage civic participation in the Black community. It educates, organize and mobilizes citizens to view civic participation as a cultural responsibility and tradition. This organization envisions a nation in which all people have the tools to fully participate in the democratic process at the local, state, and national levels. Its organizers fight to eliminate barriers to civic participation and promote greater social and economic justice.

Black Lives Matter (BLM) was founded in 2013. It's a global organization in the U.S., U.K. and Canada. Its mission is to eradicate White supremacy and build local power to intervene in violence inflicted on Black communities. The BLM movement has been instrumental in organizing protest following the death of George Floyd.

Japanese American Citizens League (JACL) is a national organization whose mission is to secure and safeguard the civil and human rights of Japanese Americans and Pacific American community. They work to promote cultural, educational and social values and preserve the heritage and legacy of the Japanese-American community.

Chinese-American Planning Council (CPC) is one of the largest non-profit providers of educational, social, and community services for Chinese American community. They service over 8,000 daily through some 50+ programs at over 30 locations. CPC's mission is to service Chinese American immigrants and low-income communities.

Asian American and Pacific Islander (AAPI): Organized during 1982, AAPI communities consist of about 50 ethnic groups speaking over 100 languages, with connections to Chinese, Indian, Japanese, Filipino, Vietnamese, Korean, Hawaiian, Pacific Islander and other Asian cultures. Over 24 million Americans or 7.3% of the U.S. population are AAPI members. The mission of AAPI are as follows:

To ensure that legislation passed by the U.S. Congress, provides for the full participation of Asian Americans and Pacific Islanders and reflects the concerns and needs of the Asian American and Pacific Islander communities.

To educate other Members of Congress about the history, contributions and concerns of Asian American and Pacific Islanders.

To work with other Members of Congress to protect and advance the civil and constitutional rights of all Americans.

To establish policies on legislation and issues relating to persons of Asian and/or Pacific Island ancestry who are citizens of, or nationals of, residents of, immigrants to the United States, its territories and possessions.

To provide a structure to coordinate the efforts, and enhance the ability, of the Asian American and Pacific Islander Members of Congress to accomplish those goals. Discussions are healthy; but actions are required for progress to take place.

There is one group, Ku Klux Klan (KKK), who caused more harm than good to promote racism.*26* This is an American White supremacist terrorist and hate group whose primary targets were African Americans, Jews, Latinos, Asian Americans, Catholics, Native Americans, homosexuals, Muslims, and Atheists. There are over 6,000 members, but are denounced by most Christian denominations.

Photo 46. The Ku Klux Klan is one of the 733 White march demonstrating their anti- America and they are still growing!

Photo 47. The KKK *is on a march demonstrating their anti-racism to the public in Alabama.*

Photo 48. There is so much hate generated by the Whites, there are other ethnic groups that are retaliating against the KKK for hate crimes.

1. *Adding Stricter Laws with Punishment that will Discourage Racism:*

It appears that increasing the severity of punishment against racism and prejudices does little to deter crime. In fact, criminal justice experts say that it may even do the opposite effects. However, being caught might be a deterrence. More research needs to be done to confirm this assumption. A large number of racial crimes are what we call expressive crimes—that is they are affected by anger, rage, depression, drug or alcohol use, indicators of psychological disturbances. With the explosion of cannabis clinics, more crimes are being created. The marijuana plant contains more than 100 different chemicals called cannabinoids—each having a different effect on the body in different ways on different individuals. Obviously more research is necessary on what marijuana does on individuals already prone to anger, rage or depression. A study done in 2018 revealed a link between racial discrimination and suicidality in African- American youths and adolescence. Another 2019 study demonstrated that socioeconomic discrimination is a robust risk factor for initiating alcohol use in young Black female youths and should be considered in the development of targeted prevention programs such as the one in the Korean American-Black American riots in Los Angeles.

J. *Organization Fighting for Equity in the Mental Health Treatment Gap:*

The Covid-19 pandemic produced at lot of Americans with depression and mental instability. No doubt that this caused a lot of racial unrest. This will continue into the future as new variants such as Deltacron variant and BA.2 to BA.5 subvariants will create even more mental health issues that can push a mentally unstable person over the edge to commit a hate crime. Do we know enough about Opioids and their effects?

Major depression was most prevalent among Hispanics (10.8%), followed by African Americans (8.9%), and White Americans (7.8%). The economic factors most strongly associated with major depression were the lack of employment and lack of health insurance coverage. The real question is does this depression have anything to do with the riots related to minority racism?

There are many mental health programs for both bipolar 1 and 2 for minorities:

Black People and African Americans

BEAM—Black Emotional Mental Health Collective

Black Mental Health Alliance

Ethel's Club

Psychology Today Directory of African American Therapist

Therapy for Black girls

African Americans, Anxiety and Depression Association of America

Black/African American, Behavioral Health Equity, Substance Abuse and Mental Health Services Administration

Black and African American Communities and Mental Health, Mental Health America

Black Mental Matters Podcast

Black Therapist Podcast

Brother You're on My Mind Toolkit, Omega Psi Phi Fraternity and the National Institute on Minority Health and Health Disparities

Minding My Black Business Podcast

The Safe Place

Sharing Hope: Speaking with African Americans About Mental Health, Nation Alliance on Mental Illness

Asian Americans and Pacific Islanders

Asian American Psychological Association

Asian Counseling and Referral Service

Asian Do Therapy

Asian Mental Health Collective

National Asian American and Pacific Islander Mental Health Association

South Asian Mental Health Initiative & Network

National Alliance on Mental Illness

Asian American Health Initiative

    The discrimination, harassment, and violence due to racism have a serious impact on the mental health and wellbeing of Asian Americans and Pacific Islanders. For example, one study found that 42% of those who had experienced discrimination had anxiety symptoms, 30% had depression symptoms, and 39% had symptom of post-traumatic stress. Thus, it is critical that these communities have easy access to appropriate mental-health resources. Racism takes a serious toll on the mental health of an individual. According to the American Psychological Association, individuals who experience hate crimes in the form of verbal harassment or physical attacks, hate graffiti, looting, burning of property, harming children of color are more likely to experience:

Anger

Anxiety

Depression

Post-traumatic syndrome

K. *Changing Gun Laws:*

Guns have been a menace to the American society. The U.S. is the only Country with more guns than people (Nearly 400 million firearms in civilians' hands). Four in 10 adults have registered firearms.[7] What about the millions of guns that are not registered by Americans? Gun ownership is still on the rise. Understandably, we do not want our 2nd Amendment to the United States Constitution (The right to keep and bear arms) taken away from us. Many Americans view hunting as a sport. However, why should it be legal for the average American to own a semi-automatic or automatic assault weapons like: Why should people have the privilege to own semi-automatic or automatic assault weapons like the following? For example:

DDM 4 V7

AK-47

PTR

Ruger Mini-14

Colt 6920 (Font size should be 14)

Remington 750

FN SCAR

Photo 49. Over the last decade, policemen have required by many states to take classes again for retraining to reduce hate crimes by being more civilized when arresting a suspect.

Dave Lange provided a long list of police who carelessly shot individuals in Cleveland wrongfully and got sued by the victims. For example, Timothy Russell and Malissa Williams were killed in a fusillade of bullets and received $3 million to Ohio when James Williams was shot by city's police while a forcible entry into her apartment. These types of senseless shootings need to stop? Is it due to anger? A Canton policeman has filed for a federal lawsuit against the officer and the city. In September 2020, Louisville, Kentucky reached a $12 million settlement with the family of Breonna Taylor, who was shot to death by the police.8 According to Richard Thompson Ford8, the George E. Osborn Professor of Law at Stanford Law School, ideas developed during the civil rights movement have been astonishing successful in the fight against overt discrimination, but can they combat the whole spectrum of social injustice—including conditions that aren't directly caused by bigotry? He argues that extremists on both sides of the political divide have hijacked civil rights for personal advantage, diverting our attention from serious social injustices. Is equality really served by endless litigating and legislating against every grievance or just slight grievances? Over the course of five decades the civil rights movement has come to enjoy the prestige of a national epic—its leaders are revered as heroes and as saints; its pivotal moments have become the stuff of legend and myth; its accomplishments, canonized; its guiding principles have acquired the status of scripture. Civil rights are remarkably effective against overt prejudice perpetrated by identifiable bigots. But they have proven important against today's most severe social injustices, which involve covert and repressed prejudice or the innocent perpetuation of past prejudice. Like an overprescribed antibiotic that kill beneficial microorganisms and eventually encourages resistant strains of bacteria, the civil rights approach to social justice, once a miracle cure, now threatens to do more harm than good. Of all the risks of rights gone wrong, perhaps the greatest is that the bad habits of opportunism, legalistic conceptualism, and festering ressentiment will slowly take the place of common sense to recognize injustice when it is staring us in the face, and the common decency to do something about it. Distracted by the wrong rights, we may neglect to right wrongs.

In 'Against Civility,' Alex Zamalin[38] argues that the best way to racial inequality is through "civic radicalism'—an alternative to civility found in the actions of Black radical leaders like Frederick Douglass, Harriet Tubman, Ida B. Wells, Martin Luther King, Jr., James Baldwin, Malcom X, and Audre Lorde. Civic radicals shock and provoked society. They name injustice and who is responsible for it, rather than spread the blame around, when it comes to economic inequality, racial violence, police brutality, and gender inequality. Civic radicals protest, march, strike, estate/lending agents. When civic radicals refuse to obey unjust laws and take up disruptive action, they confront levels of political, cultural, social, and economic power that moves elites to take notice and listen to their demands.

Civic radicals believe that racism is structural rather personal. Joel Spring[30] focused on the educational, legal, and social construction of race and racism. The educational policies of the English, and later the United States government, were formulated with this vision of Native Americans as inferior. Consequently, schools were created to destroy Native American culture and linguistic traditions and replace them with the English language and Anglo-American culture. The goal of the U.S. government was to remove the native Indians and provide useable land to the Indians and keep them isolated on Indian Reservations. At the end the

American government played major roles in racism because of skin color. So, the point that I'm trying to make is the local, state, and federal government played a major role in racism—especially with people of different color. We are all born FREE, but sooner or later, we lose that freedom because of the color of our skin or because of our culture. Guns have played a major role in highlighting racism. President Biding just signed an Executive Order into law to decrease "Ghost Guns" on April 11, 2022. Americans can no longer buy or sell Ghost Guns; it is now a Federal crime. Gun violence is a racial-justice issue. Black American homicide is a universal American threat. Black Americans are 14 times more likely than White Americans to die from gun homicide than their White American counterparts. The United Nations High Commissioner for Human Rights' Committed on Elimination of Racial Discrimination (CERD) called out the United States high number gun-related deaths and injuries, which disproportionally affect members of racial and ethnic minorities, particularly African Americans. CERD then urged the U.S. government to take action, including implementing universal background check for all private sales, prohibiting a person to carry concealed weapon (CCW) in public. It appears that this issue is getting worse with time. The public is even contemplating of protecting their family by purchasing guns themselves! Currently the following states permit the CCW certificate:

Alabama

Alaska

Arizona

Arkansas

Colorado

District of Columbia

Florida

Idaho

Illinois

Indiana

Iowa

Kansas

Kentucky

Louisiana

Maine

Michigan

Minnesota

Mississippi

Missouri

Montana

Nebraska

Nevada

New Hampshire

New Mexico

North Carolina

North Dakota

Ohio[9]

Oklahoma

Oregon

Tennessee

Texas

Utah

Virginia

Washington

West Virginia

Wisconsin

Wyoming

The Ohio House is set to pass legislation today (March 2, 2022) to allow people in the state of Ohio to carry a concealed handgun without permit, and no longer require them to proactively inform law enforcement during a traffic stop that they're armed. Senate Bill 215, which passed out of a House Committee on enforcement, is going to create a stir. President Joe Biden has yet to sign any significant new gun control bills into law. Presently there were 98,927 people that renewed their licenses in Ohio. CCW permits in Ohio are good five years before they need to be renewed. In recent years, the Ohio General Assembly has chipped away at requirements on Americans own more guns per capita than any other country in the world. There were 3.4 million deaths due to firearms in 2021. A key issue is the recognition how society distinguishes gun violence in White, suburban neighborhoods (i.e., Mass shooting in schools, malls, and streets) benefits or lack of benefits of permit-less CCW is too early, Jerry Petzer [10] states that there are flaws in many of the studies. For example, many studies were done by gun proactivist secretly sponsored to produce bias conclusions. Also, many of the studies were ill-designed or measured different endpoints like effects on suicides. He did find three studies whereby the hate crimes did rise after passing the permit-less CCW law. Laura Robertson-Boyd, a volunteer with the Ohio Chapter of Moms Demand Action for Gun Sense in America, noted that since Alaska and Arizona passed permit-less carry bills in 2010, the rate of aggravated assaults committed with guns in Alaska was up by 92% and 52% in Arizona by 2019. One 2020 study by Florida State University criminologist, Emma Fridel, found that firearm homicide rates in "shall issue" and permit-less carry states are almost 11% higher than in "may issue" states. A separate 2019 study led by Donohue states that their data analysis shows that state "right to carry" laws increase in violent crime of 13-15% after 10 years, with positive but not statistically significant effects on property crime and murder. Donohue said, "gun-rights groups muddy the waters by funding studies showing that relaxing gun laws reduces crime, though he added it's little hard to know how much that's the case because researchers don't always reveal the nature of their findings."

L. *Establish Diversity in the Work Environment:*

One of the many ways that we can reduce discrimination is by creating work environments that establish ethnic diversity. What is unique about Asian Americans is that they are well represented in the workforce, yet woefully underrepresented in the corridors of corporate power--they hit a "bamboo ceiling" just as women are said to be blocked by a glass ceiling when trying to get to the corporate ladder. A lot of different organizations are hiring their first diversity officer ever. We only want someone Black or Brown. Debbie Tang, a partner at Bridge Partners, a New York-based executive search firm specializing in finding candidates from diverse groups for leadership roles. "That's what people think of when they think of diversity. It is hard to get them to understand that Asian Americans are a minority too. To understand why the Asian American are experiencing growing numbers of perpetrators. For example, many are blaming individuals and races like former President Donald Trump and his administration for triggering the attacks by referring to COVID-19 as the "Kung Flu" and "China virus." Anti-Asian hate crimes rose from 164 to 195 incidents in 16 of the Country's largest cities the first quarter of 2021 compared with the same period in 2000, according to the Center for the Study of Hate and Extreme at California State University. During 2000, anti-Asian hate crimes surged 146 percent. The anger, which reached a boiling point during March of 2021 after the killing of six Asian descent women in Atlanta, Georgia. This hate crime sparked unparalleled activism in the almost 11% higher than in "may issue" states. A separate 2019 study led by almost 11% higher than in "may issue" states. A separate 2019 study led by community that went beyond protests and petitions.

Photo 50. Many demonstrations and riots like this one occurred throughout America. As time goes by, it is getting more frequent and more violent.

In May, prominent Asian Americans business executives like Sheila Marcelo, the founder of Care.com and Jerry Yang, co-founder Yahoo, pledged $125 M to start a new nonprofit—the Asian American Foundation to increase the community's influence and economic status. Earlier, a coalition of Asian-American business leaders, including Zoom CEO Eric Yuan and OpenTable CEO Debby Soo, bought a full-page ad in *The Wall Street Journal* to condemn the brutality and pledged $10 million to fight it--"We are tired of being treated as less than American, subject to harassment and now, every day, we read about another member of our community being physically attacked, simply for being Asian." Politicians are paying attention—In May 2022, President Joe Biden signed the COVID-19 Hate Crimes Act, which is designed to combat attacks against Asian-Americans by raising awareness and expediting review of potential hate crimes at all levels of government. This followed other initiatives, including the appointment of a Deputy Assistant to the President who will serve as liaison to the Asian American and Pacific Islander community with 24 million people in the U.S. with full or partial Asian heritage or 7% of the American population. The Society for Human Resource Management research found that over the last year,

17 percent of Asian-American workers felt that they were treated unfairly because of their race or ethnicity. Among the S&P 500 companies, there are 29 CEOs of Asian descent (5.8 percent), and 25 of them are male.[2]

Photo 51. These 5-star Asian American chefs developed a super restaurant that employed multi-cultural helpers that the entire community enjoyed. We need more of these types of creative restaurants to reduce hate crimes!

Research shows that all minority-owned small businesses suffered more than their White-owned counterparts, yet the substantial problems faced by Asian-American small-business stood out because they contrast sharply with the group's previous experiences.[35] Ninety percent said their revenue shrank in the 12 months ending in September 2020, according to AARP. About 85% of Black owned businesses, 80% of Hispanic-owned businesses, and 76% of White-owned businesses endured similar losses. Nearly 9 out of 10—of firms owned by Asian Americans reported having financial challenges last year, up from 70% in 2019. Meanwhile, 92% of Black- owned firms said that they were experiencing financial stress, up from 85% in 2019. During 1945, the town of Waterloo, Iowa and other states across the Country had blocks of real state that was kept all White by setting up barriers by barring the sale of homes to members of any ethnic groups.[11] A half a century later, Black American households headed by a falling further behind, even if no further discrimination piles on. Lower property appraisals biased loan denials, real estate agents steering clients to or away from that are associated with alpha males. Despite the progress of trying to come up with more middle managers and more executives, the statistics on business and neighborhood based on their race were many of the tactics used in the industry to stop contamination of the neighborhood by color.

The Japanese-Americans were highly praised during the 1960s for overcoming the prejudice and internment they faced during World War II and disparaged the Black community for failing to thrive. The Japanese descent were praised for their respect for authority, academic excellence, and subordination of the individual to the group. Over the years, that adulation metamorphed into a stereotype by which all Asians were painted as: neighborhood based on their race were many of the tactics used in the industry to stop contamination of the neighborhood by introducing people of color. The Japanese-Americans were highly praised during the 1960s for overcoming the prejudice and internment they faced during World War II and disparaged the Black community for failing to thrive.

Hardworking

Smart and creative

Respectful

Law abiding

Humble

55% of Asian-American responders in a survey said business has done very little in the way of concrete actions to address systemic racism. 67% believe business has largely ignored the problems of racism against their community.

58% of Asian-American respondents say racism in the workplace damaged their relationship with their employer.

Had respect for authority since Equal Pay Day was introduced in 1996 to mark the day when women caught up to the wages of White, non-Latino men earned the year before, the U.S. has improved on pay disparity by just 8 cents.[12]

Many companies are trying to expand the idea of what skills and characteristics make a good manager, though they are still fighting against a long-ingrained belief that traits such as aggression and competitiveness are adjectives that can promote racism is still grim because it is the TRUTH!

M. *Have the Churches Play a more Critical and dynamic Role in the Community to Reduce Asian-American Racism?*

The churches have to play a more active and dynamic role in *antiracism*. Based on the teachings of the Bible; we need to enforce the following[17]:

Symptoms for Unforgiveness[20]:

You bring your anger and bitterness into every relationship

You become so wrapped up in the wrong that you cannot enjoy the present

You become depressed and anxious and cause hate crimes

You feel that your life lacks meaning or purpose, or that you're at odds with your spiritual • beliefs

You lose the joy of Love for the Lord and for others

There are Seven Steps to Forgiveness20:

1. Acknowledge the hurt and anger that you have created to others:
    a. Consider how the hurt and pain have affected you; just think how the other victims also feel.
    b. Do on to others, as you want others to do onto you; we all want to feel happy with joy and not hurt and sadness.
    c. We need to learn to forgive more.

Photo 52. You have a choice of EMOTION: Positive or Negative

Photo 53. People of mixed colors working together harmoniously. This is the America that we should all be striving for in the future.

2. Accept that you cannot change the past, but you can change the present, and God will change the future.

3. Acknowledge how your wicked actions have hurt God—your savior.
4. Release yourself from the emotional prison and make a determination to forgive.
5. Repent
6. Continue to pray to receive God's support and grace.
7. Spread the forgiveness to all mankind.

There are three types of Forgiveness[20]:

1. *Exoneration* — Essentially means that the slate is completely wiped cleaned and the relationship is fully restored to its previous sense of innocence. *"To forgive and to forget."*
2. *Forbearance* — This is a second level forgiveness, which is a partial forgiveness. It is an apology suggesting that the other person is partially to blame for the wrongdoing.
3. *Release* — This is the lowest level of forgiveness, which applies to situations in which the person who hurts you has never acknowledged any wrongdoing. He or she either never apologized or has offered an incomplete or insincere apology. Apology or not, no reparations have been given and the perpetrator has done little or nothing to improve the relationship:[20]

"All bitterness, fury, anger, shouting, and reviling must be removed from you, along with all malice."

Ephesians 4:31-32

"When you stand to pray, forgive anyone against whom you have grievance, so that your heavenly Father may in turn forgive your transgressions.

Mark 11:25

"Then Peter came to Jesus and asked, 'Lord, how many times shall I forgive my brother or sister who sins against me? Up to seven times?' I tell you, not seven times, but seventy-seven times."

Mathew 18:21-22

The churches should take a more active role against anti-racism, antidiscrimination, and anti-prejudices by doing the following:

Photo 54. This Black person with a handicap has enough challenges, let alone hate crimes and acts of racism. No human being should undergo teasing and taunting because of his or her physical, mental, or social handicaps.

1. *Do a small group study:* Have members of the congregation actively participate their personal experiences with hate crimes. Have one person be a facilitator to direct the meeting and a scribe to take notes so the others can concentrate on the various topics that are being discussed.

2. *Lead a small group study authored by a person of color:* You can choose a person of color that was a victim of hate crime to lead a discussion. Keep the discussion scripter based so the outcome can be different from ordinary meetings.

3. *Start a Book Club:* At your church to uncover facts and to dispel myths. The book club should make it a priority to ensure that there are sufficient kid's books so that you start the educational process at a very young age.

4. *Host a Zoom Conversation:* Don't wait until you can meet an in- person conversation when a hate crime occurs in town. The sooner the better. The incident is fresh in one's mind and the participants have stronger reaction to the crime scene.

5. *Provide a parenting class:* and cover what to teach the parents on how to teach children about race and diversity. Have the youth minister collect the

proper reading materials and books to offer to the parents on coaching their children how and what to teach about anti-racism. For instance, how do teach and celebrate diversity.

6. *Read Diverse Books to Kids:* Include the reading of diverse picture books in your children's ministry. Include books that show the importance of love to people of other colors and cultures.

7. *Take an online course on discrimination and prejudices:* to uncover the latest research findings. For example, the General Commission of Religion and Race of the United Church have videos for persons who is interested in learning and teaching others about implicit bias.

8. *Make an action Plan:* The church must take proactive measures to prepare for racialized crises. Ministers and Priests should include prayers on discrimination, prejudices, and racism. Sunday school for children should contain lessons on hate crimes—how they are non-Christian behaviors.

9. *Virtual Reality:* All children, young adults and college kids know how to communicate by virtual reality. This form of visual and audio form of education works very well and should be used abundantly when educating people about discrimination, prejudices and racism.

10. *Making friends when you retire:* While it is a tad late, you can still make friends. loneness, depression, and anxiety are common symptoms when you age. Making friends of any color so long as they turn out to be great friends, best friends, loyal friends.

According to Jim Wallis[37] racism is rooted in sin or evil; sin must be named, exposed, and understood before it can be repented. According to this pastor, one place we should start with anti-Racism is with parents— parents of students at the same school with children of different races. Nearly all parents care deeply about the education of their kids, and they want the schools their children are in to be good for them and for all their kid's classmates too. The pastor's wife, Joy Carroll, served for many years at John Eaton Elementary School in Washington, DC as president of the Home School Association, a group like the PTA and was always dealing with diversity—not just what the numbers were, but with the reality and depth of the relationships between children and parent across racial lines. Joy said diversity doesn't just happen: "What we have learned over the years is that it doesn't just happen. Even in a healthy, diverse environment like John Eaton school, we know that we must always be aware, thinking, consciously considering our life together as set in a historic culture of racism and White privilege. Within the Asian American community, there were some nasty reports that some Black nationalist groups in different cities were fabricating incidents to exploit the provocative rumors about Korean business and beliefs that all Koreans disrespected Blacks.[35] This probably why the riots in LA started a decade ago.

According to Sung Yeon Choimorrow[13] a journalist, we must end the culture of degradation and fetishizing because Asian-American women are still in danger today, March 15, 2022. She said, "Our organization just finished a first-of-its kind survey of Asian American and Pacific Islander women's safety. The results were damning: 74% of AAPI women said that they experienced racism or discrimination in the previous 12 months. More than half identify a stranger as the perpetrator, and 47% report experiencing racism and discrimination in public space. Enough is enough!

In this 21st century we need to find solutions to this pandemic problem.

According to Trevor Hughes's research[14] the Asian Americans still cannot forget about the Georgia spa killings. Many Asian Americans try to "blend in" by wearing a baseball hat. Such a shame. Instead of "blending in" they all should "speak up" about their feelings and their thoughts so Congress can make changes in the laws to prevent these hate crimes[15].

Photo 55. Of the three ski resorts that I teach in N.E. Ohio, there are only one Nisei (Japanese American) and one Black American coach; the Vail Resorts organization needs to make a concerted effort to hire more Japanese- and Black-American coaches. In fact, they need to hire people of all colors by being colorblind.

Frank James, a 62-years-old Black male, allegedly set off a smoke bomb in a New York subway on April 12, 2022 and used a Glock 9- millimeter handgun and three loaded magazines, a hatchet, fireworks, and a liquid believed to be gasoline. Ten people were shot, five victims were critical; another 13 people suffered injuries related to smoke inhalation, falls or panic attacks. Fortunately, his Glock jammed, which resulted in less bloodshed. He had a long history of crime and should have been under surveillance a long time ago. The suspect in Tuesday's subways attack appears to have posted dozens of videos on social media in recent years —lengthy rants in which he expressed a range of harshly bigoted views and, more recently criticized the policies of New York City's mayor, Eric Adams. How seriously do our government view these hate crimes in America? What is our President going to do about it? The local sheriff should be involved; including the NYPD, NY Highway Patrol, Department of Homeland Security, FBI, CIA, and Department of Defense. It is these types of negligence that needs more active monitoring to reduce hate crimes. The N train snakes through working-class neighborhoods filled with immigrants from all over Asia and Latin America. It is time that America gets off their duff and do something about these horrific and merciless crimes and start protecting the American citizens! We deserve at least that much. We are no longer the *Land of the Free*. We are captives to hateful people in the streets.

Welcome to the friendly and peaceful United States of America!

Chapter 9
Summary

Racism is a difficult topic to conquer. It is multi-factorial in its causes and it is a moving target. It has lasted for centuries. Anti- Semitism against the Jews existed 1000 years before the Common Era (BCE). After the advent of Christianity, a new anti-Judaism evolved. During the next three centuries (300-600 C.E) a new pattern of institutionalized discrimination against the jews occurred—Jews were forbidden to marry Christians (399 CE), were prohibited from holding positions in government (439 CE), and were prevented appearing as witnesses against Christians in court (531 CE). Jews were officially being ostracized from society. In 1095, Pope Urban II made a general appeal to the Christians of Europe to take up the cross and sword and liberate the Holy Land from Muslims, beginning what was to be known as The Crusades. The Crusader Army, which resembled a mob, swept through Jewish communities—looting, raping, and massacring Jews. Thus, the program, the organized targeting of Jews was born. The Holocaust (Hashoah in Hebrew) was the single-most traumatic event for the Jewish people in the 20th century. In 1933-1945, the Nazis' persecution of the Jews became a genocide. Approximately 6 million Jews and some 5 million others, were targeted for racial, political, ideological, and behavioral reasons, died in the holocaust. More than one million of those who perished were children.

According to N'dea Yancey-Bragg[16] there are over 733 hate groups in America. The Proud Boys were one of the hate groups that attacked the White House January 6, 2022. The SPLC, a liberal advocacy group, identified 72 chapters of the extremist group, the Proud Boys, last year, an alarming rise from the 43 found in 2020. Is there any hope for the future with improving anti-racism, prejudices, and discrimination of color? I'm beginning to really wonder if America has what it takes to pull together to be the *United* States under ONE nation.

Be mindful that I have just scratched the surface when it comes to race and racism. For example, I have not covered the disabled children who are teased and bullied a lot; heaven forbids if they are colored.*20* What about the amputees, the visually impaired, the hearing impaired, or the cognitively impaired? In addition, consider the multitude of hate crimes that are thrust onto the LGBTQ groups, which are a very heterogenous, diverse, and unique group of individuals. God gave all of us free will to make choices to set us free. He also gave us 10 commandments to follow to be on the correct pathway to be good citizens.

Photo 56. This child is learning sign language because of her disabilities with hearing. What about other forms of disabilities[23] like being blind, having autism or Down Syndrome, or having a stuttering issue? Will they be teased or harassed too?

Photo 57. This amputee is trying his best to learn to ski without being criticized or taunted.

Photo 58. This individual is holding a sign up to show his conviction—just as many others, including me.

Photo 59. This racism victim is showing her feelings.

Photo 60. A teen praying for peace, love, and forgiveness in church.

According to Janet Muguia, CEO of Unidos US[17], the largest national Hispanic civil rights and advocacy organization in the U.S, and Women of the Year (2022), one needs to *Move FORWARD* to have success with racism. She never did stop; the company now oversees a network of almost 300 community-based organizations that provides support related to programs in health, education, workforce, technology, home ownership, civil rights and immigration. She uses her voice to promote policies that promote the Hispanics' color of their skin or culture.

There is ***HOPE!*** When things move forward like when President Joe Biden signed into law the first bill that specified lynching as a federal hate crime—*The Emmitt Till Anti-Lynching Act*, that's progress[18]. The historic past has revealed that there were more than 4,400 documented lynching of Black Americans between 1877 and 1950. After 100 years and over 200 attempts, the law was signed into effect on March 29, 2022. It poses a penalty of up to 30 years in prison if the law is broken. We just need to protect all people with different colors and different cultures, including Asian Americans. Isn't it time we stop our barbaric nature and create an America that is filled with ***Peace, Love, and Forgiveness?*** In addition, when it comes to sexual slavery like with Lee Yong-soo, a South Korean woman who was enslaved sexually by Japan's World War II military, we need to show more civility and forgiveness. Better yet, prevent such heinous crimes despite the fact that it every war sexual slavery has been documented.

Photo 61. Crown of Thorns. Jesus Christ died for our sins—Racism and Hate Crimes—are sinful behaviors that should be eliminated from our daily learned conduct.

What needs to be understood is **Why** people *hate* and try to *injure* (Mentally or physically) others on the basis of racial or other perceived *differences*. Until one truly understands what it is that motivates such hatreds and attitudes, why they come about and in certain circumstances, where the circumstances are part of the explanation—it is impossible to understand what racism is.

The current surge in anti-Asian American hate crimes by the xenophobic rhetoric of former President Donald Trump, who has continued to refer to the COVID-19 as the "China virus," blaming that country for the pandemic. No person, not even the president of the United States should accuse a race or culture of anything—he is an example of a poor role model.

We need more science and research on the causes of race and racism in America. Why is America the leading country when it comes to violent crimes in the schools, malls, stores, streets? Are we violent people by nature? Is it because we do not have adequate laws to protect our children? Why don't we study countries with the least amount of deadly hate crimes?

LIST OF COUNTRIES WITH THE LEAST RACISM IN 2022

Country	Ranking
Netherlands	1
Canada	2
New Zealand	3
Sweden	4
Denmark	5
Finland	6
Switzerland	7
Norway	8
Belgium	9
Austria	10

France	
11	
Ireland	
12	
Australia	
13	
Portugal	
14	
Greece	
15	

According to the International Convention on the Elimination of all forms of Racial Discrimination (CERD) the United States is ranked 69th out of 78 countries. Why so much hatred and racism? We need to more research with the countries with the least racism are doing right. The hate crimes and racism must stop in America—*Now!* We must protect our precious resources—*OUR KIDS!* Look at what happened at Roon Elementary School in Texas. We need to build better protection plans including the elimination of semi-automatic weapons, double closed entrance doors with cameras, better arrest laws and gun laws and better mental health and stability screening.

Figure 5. Fathom—Mankind can, indeed, be evil and will pose a constant challenge.

ALOHA (WITH LOVE) & MAHALO (THANK YOU)

Photo 62. **Ultimate Goal:** *Children of different races playing harmoniously throughout America.*

Photo 63. Churches generally have more mixture of different races of different skin color—that lend themselves to healthy teaching environment—of racism and hate crimes.

Photo 64. Interviewing Miss Chinatown of San Francisco, Stephanie Lee, gave me some insight into racism among Asian Americans. Her talents and beauty resulted in less discrimination and hate crimes; she also said that there were two things that she did to prevent such behavior from bothering her: "(1) not letting it get under her skin, and (2) by carrying herself with confidence and always projecting love and kindness to everyone."

Photo 65. To eliminate racism, everyone must do their part. War veterans must forget the past and forgive their enemies. Today we still have American citizens having grudges against Japanese Americans because of WW-II. Enough is Enough; that was 80 years ago!

HAVE THE HAWAIIAN SPIRIT "NO PILIKEA"

(No Worries About Color)

We Hawaiians with the Hawaiian spirit don't care about a person's religion, skin color, dress code, how they look, or what language they speak.

TRY A NEW COVENANT "LOVE ONE ANOTHER[27] AS HE LOVED YOU"

How can I play a more active role in eliminating **Hate Crimes** in America? By removing all forms of hate thoughts in your thought process; and filling it with more *love* and *kindness*—By practicing the *ABCs of Love & Kindness* (By **A**lways **B**eing **C**ommitted to *loving* and practicing *kindness* to everyone—by sharing, giving. Complimenting, being more grateful, and smiling more.

REFERENCES

1. Alland, Jr., Alexander; Race in Mind: Race, IQ, and Other Racisms; Palgrave Macmillan; New York, NY; 2002, 219 pages.
2. Bonilla-Silva, Eduardo; Racism Without Racists: Color-Blind Racism and the Persistence of Racial Inequality in the United States; Rowman & Littefield Publishers; New York, NY; 2003, 214 pages.

3. Chang, Iris; The Chinese in America; Penguin Books; New York, NY; 2004, 496 pages.
4. Chang, Iris; The Rape of Nanking; Basic Books; New York; NY; 1997, 290 pages.
5. Chiba, Hiroko and Grepinet, Vincent; Japanese Character Writing; For Dummies; 2019, 91 pages.
6. Chou, Rosalind S. and Feagin, Joe R., The Myth of the Model Minority: Asian Americans Facing Racism (2nd Edition); Routledge Taylor & Francis Group; New York, NY; 2016, 259 pages.
7. Conrad, Richard; Culture Hacks: Deciphering Differences in American, Chinese, and Japanese Thinking; Loncrest Publishing; 2019, 445 pages.
8. Fleming, Crystal M.; How to be Less Stupid about Race: on Racism, White Supremacy, and the Racial Devide; Beacon Press; Boston MA; 2018, 230 pages.
9. Ford, Richard Thompson; Rights Gone Wrong; Farrar, Straus and Giroux; New York, NY; 2011, 258 pages.
10. Hoare, James; Korea: The Essential Guide to Customs & Culture; Kuperard Publishing; London, England; 2021, 200 pages.
11. Gillborn, David; Racism and Antiracism in Real Schools; Open University Press; Buckingham, England; 1995, 234 pages.
12. Kelly, Matthew; Life is Messy; Blue Sparrow, Pathsala, India; 1971, 154 pages.
13. Kim, Soo; Korean Writing for All; Soo and Carrots Blackwell; England, 2021, 96 pages.
14. Lee, Erika; The Making of Asian America; Simon & Schuster; New York, NY; 2015, 545 pages.
15. Lee, Min Jin; Pachinko; Grand Central Publishing; New York, NY; 2017, 527 pages.
16. Leung, Christine T.; What I See: Anti-Asian Racism from the Eyes of a Child; LegaC Publishing, Clinton, MA; 2021, 31 pages.
17. Mei, Japan; Learn Japanese Beginners Workbook: Hiragana & Katakana; Just Reality Press; Monee, IL; 2022, 143 pages.
18. Munemitsu, Janice; The Kindness of Color; Tyndale House Publishers, Carol Stream, Il; 2021, 211 pages.

19. Naito, Herbert K.; Coaching Wacky Raccoon, Children & Adults: The Fundamentals of Good Sportsmanship; Proisle Publishing Service, New York, NY; 2022, 32 pages.
20. Naito, Herbert K.; How God Prepared & Inspired Me to Be A Writer & Author; Proisle Publishing Service, New York, NY, 2022, 20 pages.
21. Naito, Herbert K.; A Comprehensive Guide for Coaching Children How to Ski; Proisle Publishing Service, New York, NY, 2022, 183 pages.
22. Naito, Herbert K.; How to Create Fun for Children with Disabilities on the Ski Slopes; Proisle Publishing Service, New York, NY, 2022, 80 pages.
23. Naito, Herbert K.; How to Create Successful Ski Lesson Plans for Senior Citizens; Proisle Publishing Service, New York, NY, 85 pages.
24. Norbury, Paul; Japan: The Essential Guide to Customs & Culture; Kuyperard Press, London, England, 200 pages.
25. Ong, Henrick and Ong, Selvia; Chinese Character Practice Book; Colossal Press, Chicago, IL.; 2021, 200 pages.
26. Park, Carol; Memoir of a Cashier: Korean Americans, Racism, and Riots; Chass Int, Riverside, CA; 2017, 157 pages.
27. Rev. Kersten, John C.; New Catholic Sunday Missal; Catholic Book Publishing Corp; New Jersey, 1586 pages.
28. Reynolds, Jason and Kendi, Ibram X.; Stamped: Racism, Antiracism, and You; Little, Brown and Company; New York, NY; 2020, 294 pages.
29. Spring, Joel; Deculturalization and the Struggle for Equality: A Brief History of the Education of Dominated Cultures in the United States; McGraw Hill; Ney York, NY; 2004, 128 pages.
30. Townsend, Carole; Blood in the Soil: A True Tale of Racism, Sex, and Murderer in the South; Skyhorse Publishing; New York, NY; 2016, 209 pages.
31. Saad, Layla F.; Me and White Supremacy: A Guided Journal to Combat Racism, Change the World, and Become a Good Ancestor; Sourcebooks; Naperville, IL; 2020, 238 pages.
32. Steinhorn, Leonard and Diggs-Brown, Barbara; By the Color of Our Skin: The Integration and the Reality of Race; A Plume Book, New York, NY, 299 pages.
33. Soto, Mancho; South Korea 101: The Culture, Etiquette, Rules and Customs; Mancho Soto Publishing, Las Vegas, NV, 61 pages.

34. Spring, Joel; Deculturalization and the Struggle for Equality: A Brief History of the Education of Dominated Cultures in the United States (4th Edition); McGraw Hill; New York, NY; 2004, 128 pages.
35. Van Ausdale, Debra and Feagin, Joe R.; First R: How Children Learn Race and Racism; Rowman & Littlefield Publishing Group, Inc.; Lanham, MD; 2001, 240 pages.
36. Webster, Merriam; The Merriam-Webster Dictionary; MerriamWebster, Inc., Springfield, MA; 2005, 701 pages.
37. Willis, Jim; America's Original Sin: Racism, White Privilege, and the Bridge to a New America; Brazos Press; Grand Rapids, MI; 2011, 2018 pages.
38. Zamalin, Alex; Against Civility: The Hidden Racism in Our Obsession with Civility; Beacon Press Books; Boston, MA; 2021, 175 pages.
39. Zia, Helen; Asian American Dreams: The Emergence of an American People; Farrer, Straus and Giroux; New York, NY; 2000, 356 pages.

"Whether Discrimination is baseD on race, or creed or color, or land of origin, it is utterly contrary to the american iDeals of Democracy"

President Harry S. Turman

Photo 66. A White Dove with an Olive twig symbolizes Peace and Friendship. This should be our ultimate goal in life while on this planet while dealing with race, racism, and hate crimes.

Notes

[←1]

The New York Times; June 28, 2019.

[←2]

www.hawaii.edu/diversity

[←3]

N'dea Yancey-Bragg; USA Today, Monday March 7, 2022, page 5A.

[←4]

Kim Tong-Hyung; Time Running Out for S. Korean Slavery Victim Seeking Justice; The Vindicator [Youngstown, Ohio]; Tuesday, March 22, 2022; page 2.

[←5]

Trever Hughes; Japanese Americans recall horrors of 1942; USA Today; Thursday, February 24, 2022; Page 1A & 8A.

[←6]

Dylan Wells; Lawmaker Fear New An -Asian Wave; USA Today; Tuesday, February 22, 2022, Page 1A and 6A.

[←7]

Trevor Hughes; Japanese Americans Recall Horrors of 1942; USA Today; Thursday, February 24, 2022; Page 1A & 8A.

[←8]

Jamie Smith Hopkins; Looking to Catch Up in 'An Impossible Race;' USA Today; Thursday February 24, 2022, Sec on B1.

[←9]

Jerry Pelzer; House is poised to eliminate CCW permit requirements; The [Cleveland, Ohio] Plain Dealer; Wednesday, March 2, 2022, page A1.

[←10]

Jerry Pelzer; CCW permit renewals hit a record high in 2021; The [Cleveland, Ohio] Plain Dealer; Wednesday, March 2, 2022, page 3A

[←11]

Jamie Smith Hopkins; Looking to Catch Up in 'An Impossible Race;' USA Today; February 24, 2022; pages 1A & 2A.

[←12]

Chabeli Carrazana; Equal Pay Day Sheds Light on Gender Gap; USA Today; Wednesday March 16, 2022, page 3A

[←13]

Sung Yeon Choimorrow; Asian American women are still in danger; USA Today; Tuesday, March 15, 2022, page 7A.

[←14]

Sung Yeon Choimorrow; Asian American women are still in danger; USA Today; Tuesday, March 15, 2022, page 7A.

[←15]

Chabeli Carrazana; Equal Pay Day Sheds Light on Gender Gap; USA Today; Wednesday March 16, 2022, page 3A.

[←16]

p N'dea Yancey-Bragg; SPLC: Hate Groups Drop, but Ideas in Mainstream; USA Today; Friday, March 11, 2022, page 2A.

[←17]

, Suze e Heckney; Women of the Year: Janet Murguia—Activist Promotes Equity and Access for Latinos; USA Today; Thursday, March 24, 2022, page 1A & 2A.

[←18]

Corey Williams and Gary Fields; What Prompted the Federal An -Lynching Law?; The [Cleveland, Ohio] Plain Dealer; Wednesday , March 16, 2020l page A4.

Why Does Racism Still Exist in America with Asian Americans?

by Dr. Herbert K. Naito

book review by Barbara Bamberger Scott

"The hate crimes and Racism must stop in America – now!"

Author Dr. Naito propounds a significant view of racism, hate crimes, and discrimination at all levels as they manifest in America. He sets Hawaii as a positive exemplar for its statistically based multiculturism and proposes an effort, led by the University of Hawaii, to identify causes of, and solutions for, hate crime and racism wherever found. He devotes chapters to various immigrant groups in the US, beginning with the Chinese. Their arrival in the 1800s was based on economic factors. Those who came were hardworking men who were treated as slaves, engendering bias against them that still lingers. The Japanese migrated seeking better circumstances, with families settling, often as farmers, until World War II brought about their US internment in subhuman quarters. S till, these cultures, including Koreans who arrived later, maintain strong, respect -based standards for familial and social behaviors.

In his thought-proving book, Naito cites America's prevalent concealed carry laws as a disturbing factor in hate crimes, urging readers to unite to ensure that children will be taught anti-racist, multicultural values and to publicly decry laws allowing readily available weaponry that has facilitated deadly race -based criminal activity. With multiple university degrees and honors, the author is an internationally respected speaker on the subjects addressed here. He writes with verve and sensitivity. In addition to helpful lists of active

anti-racist organizations, Naito's text is arrayed with color photographs and offers pertinent statistics regarding the incidence of racial hatred in America and worldwide. He presents disturbing case studies of racial bullying among adults and youngsters and violence resulting from race hatred, along with the possibilities for combatting these trends for the guidance and benefit of all. Naito's diligent research and revelations will likely provide a focus for workshops and hopeful innovations among a wide readership.